"A Breath of Paris,
Preserves One's Soul"
                    VICTOR HUGO

Project Editor
VALERIA MANFERTO DE FABIANIS

Editorial Coordination
LAURA ACCOMAZZO

Graphic Layout
PAOLA PIACCO

# MY PARIS

Celebrities Talk about the Ville Lumière

Text by
ALESSANDRA MATTANZA

WHITE STAR PUBLISHERS

# Contents

MY PARIS

# Preface

Where is the source of love? When is it that you realize you have deeply fallen in love? When do you realize you can't live without that person next to you, and you keep seeing him or her everywhere, even suddenly, unpredictably? Paris easily seduces you, since the French capital is like an expert and passionate lover. It knows how not to be forgotten: it steals your heart and doesn't let you go. It marks your memories and deeply touches your soul. You can leave Paris but you can't forget it.

You happen to get lost, or may intentionally get lost wandering along the city roads heading nowhere; you may sit on a bench and read a book, let your thoughts flow among the soft waves of the Seine when some boats cross the river, or linger at the gates of a yard, a garden or an unusual park. Paris pokes through its historic buildings, and asks you to discover it by sitting at a café and watching life right in front of your eyes, or catching somebody's eye.

You let yourself go with the flow of a contemporary, peculiar "dolce vita" melting with the hectic pace of Paris hard-working buzz, without being touched by it but surviving despite time passing. The city knows history and how to live the moment; it is aware that living like, that gives you everlasting feelings, meanwhile it is not afraid of pausing, at least for a while.

In Paris you don't live for working, but you work for living. Just like classical music, that will stay unique thanks to its unchanging notes written on modern scores. Paris will never get tired of marking walls, shops, bars with its unique authenticity, when compared with some other European cities. Such a spirit owns the class and elegance the metropolis gained from its long history and tradition. It's intrinsic in its buildings, like in the Parisians way of getting dressed and moving... easy, simple, full of grace, passionate, sometimes snobbish, but still irresistible. Romanticism and love really matter here, like the cult of beauty that's not just for its own sake: it goes beyond, deepens the architectural details and the evoked emotion. The details are able to develop in a moment, like an eye watching inside a kaleidoscope and rediscovering something different in each imperceptible movement. Paris does it joyfully, conveying its everlasting wish to live and be lived, as well as a touching melancholy in sensitive or lost souls.

Paris is not just the city of the thousand lights, of the Champs-Élysées, of the Eiffel Tower lit by a multitude of lights and even more glorious at dusk since in the dark it stands out of roofs, houses, historical buildings and people life. Or of the street lamps in the large, imposing and superior boulevards overwhelmed by headlights and car, motorcycle and bike traffic, rushing people, or even of the wonderful monuments lit up all night. They seem to sculpture the city structure as if it was a wholeness of statues linked together, in a sort of beautiful dance in Wonderland.

Paris comes to life from moments and feelings you can breathe in its less known alleys, in the flair of a café or a typical bistro where time has stopped and people read their papers, have coffee, chat and speculate about philosophical, political, scientific and literary ideas. Actors run lines with some friends, mothers take their kids to have hot chocolate, some tourists set off to discover some local flavor, a crêpe or an omelette... Paris is like a great illusionist, it knows how to enchant and involve, how to make you feel special, as if we were a universal whole, transfiguring images and emotions, shades of shadows. The wind chases running clouds over an overwhelming field of grey sky, that makes the city fascinating by wrapping it in an intimate, rarefied romantic atmosphere.

Paris is a city that keeps living on a horizontal level rather than on a vertical one. It's scarcely familiar with the arrogance of the really high skyscrapers. It prefers wavering in tiny daily pictures, street life, delicious smells of bakeries, bistros, brasseries, butcheries, as if they were charming mermaids... And harmony rises from its people: the Parisians want to enjoy life and have absorbed all the other cultures thanks to their clever curiosity, shaping a fantastic mixture of colors and traditions, between history and the future.

Paris wavers between memory images and visions. The past – to be known, in order to deeply love the city – reflects its important history, able to change the world destiny. You can breathe it in its elegant buildings and rediscover it in its culture pervading huge museums, numerous theaters and cinemas, as well as

ideology and intellectual spirit. The present keeps trying to assert itself and pops in the modern buildings well suitable with the existing structures and willing to open to experiments and ideas, still in accordance with traditions, though.

Paris doesn't match with thousands of colors, but endless shades of colors like gray, white, beige and brown. They are the colors of the stones of buildings and houses playfully evolving within daylight. At times, they blend with the green of the trees, the parks, the gardens, or with the sparkly hues of dresses winking from a boutique shop windows. At night, the city is overwhelmed by a bright atmosphere of lights: street lamps, headlights, window lights turning off one by one and hiding many stories to tell.

Paris keeps being the home and inspiring muse of lots and lots of artists and creative people who currently get here or live here wishing to fulfill their dreams. The purpose of this book is to gather the mind and soul of those who help this city become so special and precious. They shape Paris with extraordinary architecture, refine it with artistic, fashion, gastronomy, painting, graphics inventions, describe it in a film or in a book, in works of art, making Paris eternal and unforgettable. They contribute to create a rich, articulated, complex, hence, even more beautiful, interesting, immortal place. Here the city can be deeply fascinating indeed, made up of life moments, memories, visions, dreams, life mirrors and unique experiences.

# Introduction

A rose petal for ever lying on your heart, nourishing it as if it was the essence of its scent, of its beauty, of its sap becoming part of your own soul. Fleshy and sensual, rich in shapes and suggestions, like an orchid arousing senses. This has always been my Paris. Romantic, as sensory emotion is so intense here, like in no other city.

Paris is a city you can feel in your skin, it runs in your blood, touches your soul. You can perceive it, intense, in your nostrils: you can smell it. It overwhelms you with endless, colorful life and street scenes. Its buildings and amazing monuments leave you breathless...

Paris seduces and involves you in an enchanting love story full of melancholy, and makes it impossible to stay immune. Sometimes, I happen to think of the city when I'm far away and the first image coming to my mind is when I last saw Paris; like in an old Polaroid snapshot, faded because of the passing time. The image is always different: it may be connected to a building watched through a taxi window in a rainy day, just before leaving the city center; or to the neon sign of a brasserie I can still taste some of its dishes in my mouth; a subway station where I happened to spot two lovers kissing; a *bateau-mouche* crossing the Seine and passing under a bridge; a hotel window from where you can see the Eiffel Tower framed as in a painting; or the corner of an alley where a curious cat is peeping out...

It's as if this city was able to build a photo album in my mind. It occasionally reminds me that I should come back to watch it again and again, to shield precious memories. Who knows, one day I might stay here forever, as a part of that same collection, since I've established a bond with Paris, a connection that nothing will change.

I've lived in Paris many times, mostly in hotels; once in one of my dear French friends' attic in Saint-Germain-des-Prés, few steps far from Saint-Germain boulevard. At this time of my life, I often come back here for work and for pleasure, to meet friends, to write a book... And despite having traveled a lot, no place is able to enthral my imagination like Paris. When I'm here, it's as if I invented my self again and again, and there would be no other dimension. It's a sentimental combination left undone; it doesn't want to end, always demanding a new attempt, a new journey to enter intimacy deeply and intensively. And the feeling that draws me is irresistible, undeniable, irreversible.

The first time I saw Paris I was sixteen and it bewitched me. Not just the imposing and amazing monuments, the wide and unpredictable boulevards, a real turn-up for the books like a magic kaleidoscope where perspective changes at every corner, at every crossing, at every eye contact with passers-by; above all it was the sparkling air into my veins with a pinch of happiness in my mind, like when you taste a glass of good wine slightly going to your head.

Paris made me feel high, far away from all previous thoughts or memories, absolutely plunged in the moment. Paris had been inebriating right from the start, thanks to its interesting multitude of faces in the street, both French and foreign ones; its delicatessen in *pâtisseries* and bakeries windows; its cafés and bistros, where people would chat, share their life

# JEAN-JACQUES ANNAUD
## The "Soul Explorer"

His films dig deep into the human soul, even in animals soul as he considers them part of the magic universe mixing up Nature and humanity at the same level. A common feature of all his splendid work. The great film maker Jean-Jacques Annaud is a man who can see far ahead and inspects the world endless horizons, catching sight of those unique details he conveys in his movies. You understand that when you look into his eyes: careful, deep, intense. He chases words carefully, while he smiles lighting up his gaze even more noticeable now and framed in thick gray hair. "I've lived my latest forty years traveling all over the world on business. From set to set, I've had the chance to use my camera in exceptional places, among spectacular, far away, exotic landscapes, like the green 'ocean' of Mongolia Steppe in 'Wolf Totem' and on the Himalaya glittering mountains in 'Seven Years in Tibet'. I lived in Los Angeles eight years, in Yaoundé one year, in Rome one year and then Montreal, Saigon, Berlin, Siem Reap. I also spent two years in Munich, three in London, four in Beijing... But Paris remains 'the City', my door, my heart place", he says with a feeling making him touched, when he refers to his city. Among his movies: "Black and White in Color" (1976) winning the Golden Globe as best foreign movie in 1977, "The Name of the Rose" (1986), "The Lover" (1992). In 2007 he became a member of the Académie des Beaux-Arts in Paris.

He was born in Juvisy-sur-Orge on 1st October 1943. He was animated by a vocation for cinema, right from the start. He was fascinated by history and literature and he attended the École technique de photographie et de cinéma in Paris, now called École Louis-Lumière, and The Institut des hautes études cinématographiques (IDHEC), now Fémis.

He has also explored universes different from an artist and intellectual's conventional ones... an inspiration that has kept him bewitched throughout all his production.

"Apart from meeting human species daily, I like setting off, discovering and facing other forms of life: plants and animals. At the end of my teenage, I made an effort to analyze the ideal of the French intellectual: dry and cerebral. I kept studying ancient Greek and Medieval History at Sorbonne amphitheaters soaked in wax smell, a few steps far from the pigeons and the graceful mothers of Luxembourg gardens. I took the D2 chair at the Cinémathèque français of Palais de Chaillot all evenings during my cinema school years. And then I was sent to the heart of black Africa for my

> I live in Paris as if
> I was inside one of the city
> postcards they made
> me dream during
> my suburban childhood.

View of **Notre-Dame** Cathedral from the Seine, with Jean-XXIII square vegetation wrapping the church apse.
The **Notre-Dame** chimeras were made by Eugène Voillet-Le-Duc, who restored the cathedral between 1843 and 1864.

military service. It was compulsory at that time. My life changed: a window opened my inner jungle, far less tidy than the French gardens raked boulevards. My professional life took an unexpected turn. My first full-length film 'Black and White in Color' is inspired by a Cameroon colonial history real fact. Then I shot other films as 'Quest for Fire', set in Homo Sapiens prehistory, or 'The Bear', where the main actors are plantigrades (supposed to be less evolved than Hollywood stars...). More recently, 'Wolf Totem' starring sharp fangs quadrupeds. All my movies talk about wildlife in some way, even the one on the monks abbey 'The Name of the Rose' or the one on Stalingrad chaos and manhunt 'Enemy at the Gates'", he says.

Jean-Jacques is fond of animals and able to deeply understand their behavior, as he shows in the beautiful film "Two Brothers" where he tells the story of two baby tigers that grow up between adventures and escapes: a movie representing great ethical teaching and questioning human behavior. Among his international successes, "Wolf Totem" is based on a really particular pack fighting for survival... "If you were born again, which animal would you like to be? A man, again. Or a flying man. No, actually: a flying woman, capable of giving birth

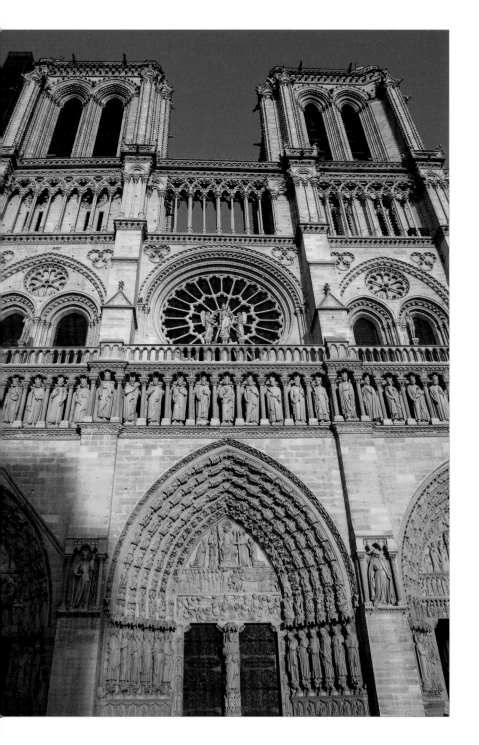

and flying over the landscape staring at the horizon. I would build my nest on a plane tree, somewhere in Paris", being ironic with his sharp and arousing spirit.

"Unlike many other metropolis changing by blows from concrete, becoming globalized and replaceable, Paris has kept its proud uniqueness", he underlines. "I can't see much difference from when I was a child in Paris, except from the fact that the city is cleaner and more lively. The blacken facades have been polished and have recovered their original, light and shiny hues. In our country there is a natural taste for continuity, an instinctive respect for the events of the past, still relevant in our view. France remains the first tourist destination in the world for having consolidated its peculiar art of life. Despite the disorders the country has to face, in France there is a general consent on maintaining landscapes, architectures, gastronomy, language, the relationship with sexuality" he explains referring to a life style and a particular national identity.

**Notre-Dame**
Notre-Dame de Paris Cathedral main facade, with the Portal of the Last Judgment, the Gallery of Kings, the rose window, the mullioned windows and the two towers.

**Gothic Outburst**
Portray of the well known painting "The Coronation of Napoleon", by Jacques-Louis David, the inside of Notre-Dame is a supreme example of French Gothic architecture.

"My favorite places in town? My favorite district is the one I have the opportunity to live in: the historical district around l'Île de la Cité. One of the Seine islands where the city was founded. In this few hectares area there is the Notre-Dame Cathedral, the Conciergerie castle-fortress (once residence of the Kings of France), the Palais de Justice and a magnificence of Gothic art, the Sainte-Chapelle. My apartment, placed on the left side of the river, is an extension of the iconic Pont Neuf, the most ancient bridge of the city. I like walking in the evening, looking at the barges under the Passerelle des Arts and the boat tours lighting up Palais de la Monnaie facades, the National mint and the Institut de France", he says. "The view stretches from Pointe du Vert-Galand to Saint-Germain-des-Prés abbey from my windows, from Louvre roofs to the golden dome of the Acadèmie Française, to the Eiffel Tower. I live in Paris as if I was inside one of the city postcard they made me dream during my suburban childhood."

What really fascinates him is Paris set of different universes and microcosms. "I love the diversity of the districts, like villages, composing the capital, with their unusual specialties shops, bistros, art galleries, numberless museums, and cinemas

**The Jardin du Luxembourg**
The pond in the middle of the big public park, often crossed by sailboat models has always been a child's ride.

Scenes of daily life in the **Marais** district, with its small and mainly Jewish shops.
**Marais** is known as one of the most fashionable areas of Paris, and among the main districts of Paris night life.

displaying the most diversified programming", he confesses. He is really fond of a glimpse he likes going to on his own. "A place I'm particularly attached to is the Jardin du Luxembourg, a park with French-style gardens surrounding the Senate home palace. Built in 1612 on Maria de Medici's request, it's attended by lovers, mothers with their strollers, retired people reading papers on benches, children sailing their boats in the ponds, tourists taking pictures in front of the statues placed in the middle of flowerbeds. It's a real heaven of peace, ideal to be on your own and reflect, possibly before going back to work"

he says with all the attention to details you can grasp in his films, full of a real artist's mastery.

His creative vein is magically stimulated by the French capital, by its awesomeness and charm, like a seductive woman's ones. "I think Paris is like Venice and Angkor, one of the most romantic places all over the world. Each time I see it after being back from a journey, or even when I come back home after an appointment, I walk the cobblestoned roads of my district and my heart is struck by emotion. I say to myself, deep down: 'What happiness, what a privilege it is to live here'."

## LES PAINS

Pains
au
cumin

Pains
au
pavot

Razowy

Rogalik

Bagels

Pletzels

Halès

## LES DOUCEURS

### VATROUCHKAS AU FROMAGE

Traditionnelle
Light
au Citron
au Griottes

### STRUDELS

Viennois
Roumain
Mame Strudel
au Pavot

### AU CHOCOLAT

Reine de Saba
Sacher torte
Brownie
Négus

sacha finkelsztajn

SACHA FINKELSZTAJN

la boutique jaune

# TRAITEUR

## SPECIALITES YIDDISH

01.42.72.78.91

RECOMMANDÉ PAR
Le Pudlo
PARIS
2002

# JANE BIRKIN

## The Muse

When beauty frames talent, grace and elegance, a refined and sharp intelligence, a special sensitivity only few artists have... then a muse is born. Jane Birkin represents all these elements, splendid as a portrait where there is no imperfection though looking for it. "If I imagine to identify Paris with one color, I think about its buildings therefore many, infinite and tiny shades of gray...", she says. "I've got several memories of Paris. The first and greatest one is when I was sixteen, maybe, while I was ending my school year. I lived in an apartment along the Bois de Boulogne together with some English girls, for a while. There Edith Piaf used to live as well and I still remember the day she died.... there was a long queue out there and and there were police. I showed my document and they let me pass, and people started whispering 'that's Françoise Hardy' and I was so happy as I had just bought her album 'Tous Les Garçons et Les Filles'", she remembers, with a vein of melancholy in her voice.

She was born on 14th December 1956 in London. Daughter of a beautiful actress, Judy Campbell and of David Birkin, a Royal Navy officer, who worked in clandestine operations together with the French Resistance. Jane started working when she was seventeen. At that time she met John Barry, the composer of the musical comedy "Passion Flower Hotel", where she played in 1965. They fell in love and got married soon after. in 1967 Kate Barry, their daughter was born. When she was twenty, she was noticed and gained a worldwide success thanks to the movie "Blow-up" by Michelangelo Antonioni. Pierre Grimblat was shooting "Slogan" and looking for a girl to give a part to placing side by side to Serge Gainsbourg. He was already famous and hadn't recovered yet from breaking up with the actress Brigitte Bardot. When Jane showed up at the audition, she could hardly speak any French and didn't know anything about Serge. She was restless and ended up bursting into tears in front of the camera. Partly due to emotion, partly because of the crisis she was living with John Barry, who then she divorced... Her spontaneous emotional reaction made her got the part. A new love was born and her destiny tied up to Paris...the mythical love affair between her and Serge started in Paris in 1969: the two became inseparable and together they recorded the song "Je t'aime moi non plus", which shocked public opinion, due to the explicit reference to a sexual intercourse. As well as selling millions of copies, the piece became the icon of that age.

> I didn't decide this would have been my city, from the start, but that's what happened.

## "I didn't intentionally choose to live in Paris. I fell in love twice... First with Serge and then with Jacques...".

"I lived with my daughter Kate, for a while. She was one year-old in 1968, we were in the 5th arrondissement, opposite Notre-Dame, in the small Hotel Esmeralda. I remember a small square near Saint-Julien-le-Pauvre Church where we used to spend time together. Then I met Serge and moved to different hotels with him and Kate...", she says.

Jane and Serge went to Yugoslavia to make "Romance of a Horsethief" by Abraham Polonsky, a film starring Yul Brynner and Eli Wallach. Nine months later, in 1971, their daughter Charlotte was born. "Di Doo Dah", Jane's first solo album was released in 1973 and she made "Seven Deaths by Prescription or Bestial Quartet" with Gérard Deparieu and Michel Piccoli, "La Moutarde Me Monte Au Nez" and "La Course à l'Echalote", Claude Zidi's popular comedies, with Pierre Richard. In 1975 Jane and Serge shot the film "Je T'Aime Moi Non Plus", becoming an exploration of homosexuality with the ambiguity of Jane as an androgynous muse. The albums "Lolita Go Home" (1975), "Ex-Fan Des Sixties" (1978) followed, and in 1983 Jane left Serge. She fell in love with the film director Jacques Doillon and in 1982 she had her third daughter with him. In films like "La Fille Prodigue" and "La Pirate", the director influenced her with his intense and dramatic style and was skilful with getting the best from the actress.

Gainsbourg suffered their separation and wrote "Baby Alone in Babylon" texts and music in 1983.

"I didn't intentionally choose to live in Paris. I fell in love twice... First with Serge and then with Jacques... And I think that's the reason I didn't go back to England in the end. I didn't decide this would have been my city, from the start, but that's what happened. I shot 'La Piscine' in the French Riviera and I was so absorbed I didn't feel like taking any kind of decisions. And then I found myself in Paris, again. I liked the Parisians, I found them funny and smart, and they liked me. They basically 'adopted' me, they wanted me to stay in their country, I had been welcomed right from the start!". Jane explains, as for choosing Paris as her own city. "I was fascinated by the Saint-Michel-Notre-Dame area and by the small and ancient bookshop 'Shakespeare and Company'. Here Stanley Kubrick used to go and do research for a film he intended to shoot, called 'Napoleon'. I used to love going there to search and read books... I had beautiful moments there...", she remembers.

In 1985 she debuted at the theater with Mariveaux's work, "La Fausse Suivante", under Patrice Chéreau's direction. In 1987 she worked out her courage to perform as a singer in a show at the Bataclan directed by Lerichomme. She had her hair cut, took singing lessons, got dressed like a man. She did that to impress Serge, as she herself acknowledges. It was a great success. In 1990 Gainsbourg dedicated his new album "Amours Des Feintes" to her. It was the last one, as Serge

Graffiti portraying Serge Gainsbourg in 5bis **rue de Verneuil**, where the artist lived between 1969 and 1991.

The **Shakespeare and Company** bookshop, in the 5th arrondissement, has been a cultural reference point since the 1920s.

died on 2nd March 1991. A few days later, her father, David Birkin's died as well and Jane was overcome with grief, as it showed at Casino de Paris stage, where pain shone through her face. She tried to commemorate Serge with all France, but after a tour ending in La Rochelle, she laid down the microphone on the stage and left... She went away from spotlights, dedicating herself to writing, her family, her dear people and humanitarian commitment. Since then she has sung for Amnesty International and cooperated with the NGO, making a short film for the fight against AIDS and directing her own film "Oh Pardon, Tu Dormais!". She also committed herself to help Sarajevo together with the association "Paris- Sarajevo-Europe".

Only after her fans' numerous requests to come back and sing Gainsbourg's music, she released her new album "Versions Jane" in 1996, where several artists reinterpreted her music. In 1998 she recorded "A la Légère", an album where she invited twelve composers to write as many original songs. Jane then continued her project. She wanted to reinterpret Gainsbourg's music, making it more accessible to the new generations and contaminating it with different genres, like Algerian, Andalusian, Gitano, Arabic ones.

**The Saint-Michel Fountain**
Carried out by the architect Gabriel Davioud between 1858 and 1860, the majestic fountain should have been decorated with a statue of Napoleon at first, but then the Archangel Michael was sculpted in it.

> "I must confess I've always found going
> to restaurants boring.
> I've always favored bars."

In 2002 she recorded the concert "Arabesque" then becoming an album. Meanwhile she worked at new records "Rendez-Vous" (2004), "Fictions" (2006) and "Enfants d'Hover" (2008). For the first time she wrote the lyrics herself. She came back to the theater with "Sophocles", directed her second film "Boxes" with Michel Piccoli and Geraldine Chaplin and played in "Around a Small Mountain" with Sergio Castellitto. She went back on stage in "La Sentinelle" a work written for her by the director and actor Wajdi Mouawad. In the social field, she committed for immigrants and backed the Burmese leader Aung San Suu Kyi. After Fukushima earthquake and nuclear catastrophe, Jane went to Japan to attend a charity concert. There he met Nobuyuki Nakajima who became the artistic director of her tour "VIA JA-PAN" celebrating the twentieth anniversary of Serge's death.

Today Jane keeps being active and prolific in her arts and within social commitment. Her Paris is full of memories.

"I've never known Montmartre well. I went there once for a funeral. The place I'm most familiar with is the Mont-

**Cafés and bistros**
The typical outdoor tables featuring Paris café and bistros represent a proper way to enjoy social relations and public, convivial environments.

**Chez Julien**
The legendary bistro is in rue du Pont Louis-Philippe, in the 4th arrondissement. Its tables have a view of Notre-Dame and provide an exclusive atmosphere.

An aerial view of the **Jardin des Plantes**, the botanical garden placed in the 5th arrondissement.

martre cemetery where many well-known people are buried... I know many artists loved and lots currently adore it. I live in the 10th arrondissement, near the Jardin des Plantes, the botanical garden. I believe it's beautiful to have a garden in Paris when you have kids. But when they grow up and leave, it can be extremely sad. A full of memories comfortable apartment is definitively better. I'm the kind of person who becomes attached to things, fall in love with things. They remind me of beautiful memories, are tied up to emotion", she says. Then she remembers: "I used to go to the playground of Bois de Boulogne with my children. There is also a wonderful lake. Both Kate and Charlotte enjoyed playing and hopping on

Autumn leaves... If I go there now, melancholy strikes my heart as I cannot hear those sounds anymore. They were so familiar they used to give me happiness. I used to go to the Jardin du Luxembourg or to the Jardin des Plantes with Lou, and I go back there now with my grandchildren."

The Paris places Jane loves are linked with her memory fragments, too. The hotel (in rue des Beaux Arts) near the Fine Arts school where Oscar Wilde spent his last years is fascinating. "Serge and I used to go there very often. It's wonderful. We sang 'Je T' Aime Moi Non Plus' in the restaurant for the first time...", she says. "I adore Japanese restaurants and tea rooms. In rue de Seine in Saint-Germain-des-Prés you

can taste the best millefeuille of Paris, at Arnaud Larher, a well-known pastry chef opposite Juget-sudo, a really high-quality Japanese green tea shop. Kioko is a Japanese grocery in rue des Petits Champ. I often go there with Lou. The Japanese restaurants I love most are: the Kinugawa, in rue du Mont Thabor, where I go with Charlotte or Lou; the Hotaru in the 9th arrondissement, where I like to have lunch with my friends; Kate introduced me to the Yen, in rue Saint-Benoit at Saint-Germain-des-Prés. Here you can savor delicious Japanese pasta, and then Juan, in rue de la Pompe, a very special place, small and intimate, with a few tables and a bar. Also Kunitoraya. It's in the 1st arrondissement. I also recommend the Italian restaurant Marco Polo, in rue de Condè, Boulevard Saint-Germain (Odeon). It's run by Albano, an exquisite and welcoming person: you can go there anytime.... daytime, for lunch, for dinner, at night.... A French place I really find extraordinary, both classic and with an excellent gastronomy, is the Café Tournon in rue de Tournon, in the 6th arrondissement. Or there's the Indian district at Gare du Nord, where there are plenty of delicious Indian restaurants. You can meet many British people, used to this cuisine and to vegetarian dishes", Jane suggests referring to the gastronomy of the city. "I must confess I've always found going to restaurants boring.

**The Bois de Boulogne**
The big park stretches on 846 hectares and is the French capital green lung. You can enjoy pleasant boat trips on the Lac Inferieur.

I've always favored bars and nightclubs, though I think old-time nightclubs have disappeared. The atmosphere has really changed", she adds. "Instead I find it romantic having a picnic in Paris. If you have children, too. Preferably in the Bois de Boulogne or in the Bois de Vincennes. You can also walk your dog and then go boating on the lake... Awesome!", she suggests.

She likes going to the cinema when she has time. "Odeon is my favorite district to go to the cinema: the halls are numerous and they all have good programming", she says. "The museums in Paris are good, but you can visit a museum everywhere... Among my favorite: the Musée d'Orsay, the Louvre and the Musée de l'Orangerie. Here Monet is displayed. His works make me think of my mother. She used to love the 'Water Lilies'", she states, reconnecting with a memory path.

Jane Birkin is a fashion muse and an icon, as well. Up to the point that the well-known French luxury maison Hermès dedicated to her a bag calling it "Birkin Bag". Over the years, such item has become legendary, though Jane asked to ensure her with the ethical origin of the leather used to make it and highlighted some unpractical elements. "I've never liked going shopping on my own, but I do when I'm with my friend Gabrielle. I favor cashmere and jersey, I like wearing something original, difficult to find, or something old, out of the market... And I've always loved wearing baggy clothes and men clothes... Saint Laurent created a wonderful denim jacket I still like wearing... I also like Isabel Marant's creations. My daughters love them as well... One day I would like to create my own fashion brand. I prefer shops with a personality and those that leave you in a good mood, colorful, original, not taken for granted", she points out. "I've already made a perfume.

**The Glass Pyramid**
Since when it was inaugurated in 1989, the Louvre glass pyramid, planned by the architect Ieoh Ming Pei as the new entrance to the museum, has become a symbol of the city.

"Museums in Paris are good, but you can visit a museum everywhere... Among my favorite: the Musée d'Orsay, the Louvre and the Musée de l'Orangerie. Here Monet is displayed. His works make me think of my mother. She used to love the Water Lilies."

The **Musée de l'Orangerie** displays important Impressionist and post-Impressionist works of art.
**"Water Lilies" by Monet**: the big panels have been shown at the Musée de l'Orangerie since 1927.

I wanted it to have the scent of memory, musk, Istanbul markets, English mansion, Paris. I wanted it to enclose familiar nuances...."

Jane gives her own advice to discover the city she adores: "A unique and cheap alternative to discover Paris is to go to the catacombs to admire the underground city. It may seem disturbing, but it's beautiful in some way. I shot an entire film down there. You can follow a path from Denfert-Rochereau in the 15th arrondissement to the Trocadero and the Eiffel Tower."

But what strikes Jane about Paris is the air she breathes: "I don't often go to London. I love British people, they are attractive and kind. But I also like the Parisians. When I got her for the first time, I learned how to relax and take my time.

The Parisians enjoy life and I love that. They sit outdoors in parks and in the streets. When I was young I was struck by this kind of life from the start", she admits. "I will never get tired of saying that I'm fascinated by the Parisians... People of all nationalities – a variety that seems even more evident here – each one with its own features and personality: French, Russian, Italian, Spanish. People have been here for generations, and that makes an amazing mix! On the first night Serge took me to a Mexican restaurant, then to the Raspoutine, a fashionable Russian nightclub. As regarding cinema, you can find films from all over the world in Paris, even Chinese ones. It's as if everybody had a chance to be seen and had their own different rules...."

# PHILIPPE CONTICINI

## The Avant-Gard Pastry Chef

He generated innovation and revolutionized contemporary and international French fine cuisine, developing his skills and mastery especially in desserts, in pastries and in their ingredients. His mind is a tireless factory of ideas, like a work of art. In 1994, the chef and pastry chef Philippe Conticini deepened his knowledge of sweet and savory, and stood out inventing the *verrines* principle: for the first time he displayed traditionally served on a plate gastronomic specialties in a vertical and transparent container. He also aimed at arousing senses and emotions as his exquisite cuisine surprises you any time.

Just like his Paris can do. He still feels like the city is deeply rooted in tradition. "What I love best of Paris is its history. You can find it in every corner, in parks and gardens, at home. I feel it in the cruel past of place de la Concorde, in the almost forgotten ruins of Paris bastions, in the Île de la Cité, wandering along the *quais* (piers), in the view of the National Assembly, at sunrise at the Louvre, in the Louvre itself", he says, pausing and thinking of other places of his city.

> Thinking of Paris, two colors come to my mind: blue and red, the city shades.

"I love rich Parisian gastronomy, as well, the museums, all the schools, the parks, the theaters, the Jardin du Luxembourg... I adore Paris at night and the shining Eiffel Tower", he adds, describing all the facets featuring such a wonderful metropolis, and making it unique and unforgettable, just like his pastry-making art.

Conticini was born on 16th August 1963, in Choisy-le-Roi. He grew up learning the first tricks of the trade in his parents' kitchen and at the Restaurant du Rocher in Vitry-sur-Seine (Val-de-Marne), and then at the starry Restaurant du Parc a Villemomble (Seine-Saint-Denis).

In 1980 he started his apprenticeship, at Alain Dutournier's well-known restaurant Au Trou Gascon, then he took on pastry at Maxim's Roissy.

After having graduated, in 1983, he became Jacques Chibois's assistant at the restaurant of the Gray d'Albion Hotel. Two years later, he moved to the Peltier patisserie. In 1986 he opened his restaurant, La Table d'Anvers (one Michelin star), in the 9th arrondissement in Paris. Right then, he conveyed his technique best, experimenting,

> "I've always been an avant-gard,
> creative, precursor artist,...
> but I wanted my pastry-making to resemble myself."

working out something new he used to do just in savory, reducing sauces and cooking times, trying unusual tastes and using unusual dessert ingredients, such as Coke.

Following his career, his fame spread in Paris and all over the world. In 1991 the Gault et Millau magazine appointed him pastry chef of the year. In 1994, his creations ventured even more with the *verrines*. His memories run to his city: "As far as I remember, my first memories of Paris are the equestrian statues at the Champs-Élysées, place de la Concorde, and the beautiful boulevard with the perspective view on the Arc de Triomphe. And then the wonderful obelisk, an Egyptian present", he states, referring to his first absolute impression of Paris. Conticini believes that Paris is one of the most beautiful city in the world, as well as his ideal source of inspiration to convey his tastes to the entire world.

In Paris, Conticini became a culinary delight celebrity, with the intent to bring his art to a wide audience, making use of widespread tools and cooperating with big food industry brands. He also wrote many cookery books and attended TV programs (like "Jeux de Goûts" and "Le Meilleur pâtissier"), establishing the international day of contemporary pastry-making ("Des arômes et des hommes"), in 1996. He co-founded the "Art et Dessert" association and collaborated with pastry-making competitions and the "Thuriès Gastronomie Magazine", with the Petrossian caviar leading selling agency, and as a pastry chef at the Petrossian restaurant, opened in Paris in 1999. He then worked together with the well known Peltier patisserie in Paris and Tokyo, while in 2003 he trained the French team winning the Pastry-Making World Cup, in Lyon. Then he devoted to some projects, opening the catering services "Exception Gourmande" company (open until 2008) and, one year later, the Pâtisserie des Rêves, with his first boutiques in rue du Bac and in rue de Longchamp, and two more in Japan.

**Paris-Brest:** one of master Philippe Conticini's best known inventions.

Among Philippe Conticini's various creations, he introduced the idea of the choux-bun bar and reshaped the French classic pastry-making: lighter, more intense and with less sugar. His delicatessens are irresistible, especially his circle like cake Paris-Brest version (appointed 2010 best dessert by "Le Figaro" newspaper) and his Saint-Honoré.

"A special dish representing Paris? Definitively the Parisian sandwich, le *jambon beurre*, with butter and ham. That's the city archetype, since all the world knows it: the baguette", he admits. As for cakes, he's even more doubtless: "If I think of a dessert for Paris... The Paris-Brest with no doubt. It was invented in 1910 by the pastry chef Louis Durand for the maison Laffitte and is inspired by the Paris-Brest-Paris bike race. Such a great classic cake has been important in my career.

**Place de la Concorde**
Two equestrian statues coming from Marly castle, were placed in this big square in 1794. The originals are currently at the Louvre.

"My favorite districts? Marais, with its exquisite place des Vosges."

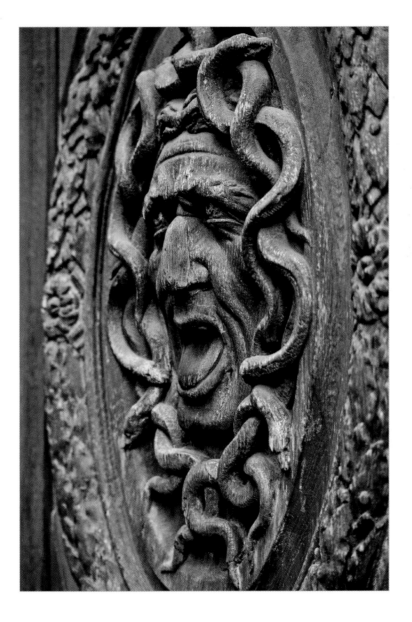

Beautiful buildings and smart hotel boutiques face **Place des Vosges**, the oldest square of Paris.

The Medusa's face is sculpted on one of the Amelot de Bisseuil Hotel wooden doors, at own-house the **Marais district**.

One of the city oldest clocks is placed on **Saint-Paul Saint-Louis church** facade, in Marais.

"What I love best of Paris is its history.
You can find it in every corner,
in parks and gardens, at home."

I've always been an avant-gard, creative, precursor artist, as the *verrines* demonstrate (his transparent and vertical dessert containers since 1994), but I wanted my pastry-making to resemble myself, simple and accessible.

That's why I reshaped French pastry-making great classics between 2008 and 2009. The Paris-Brest coincided with my most creative professional time, both for taste and technique... That's bizarre! Modern techniques like the *assaisonnement par l'air* (dressing by air) allowed me, for example, to replace the butter cream rich structure with air incorporation throughout low temperature expansion", he points out passionately.

**The Victory**
The sculptor Louis-Simon Boizot worked out a golden "Victory" to celebrate Napoleon's return from an Egyptian expedition. It's currently displayed at the Musée Carnavalet.

"Le Procope: the first true Parisian café, is in rue de l'Ancienne Comédie and shields all the French cafés and brasserie history."

**Le Procope**, in 13 rue de l'Ancienne Comédie, is the oldest café of Paris: it was established in 1686.

**The Literary Café:** French Literature great exponents are used to hanging out at Le Procope: it is one of the most popular cafés in Paris.

His Paris is like his colorful and tasteful culinary art. "Thinking of Paris, two colors come to my mind: blue and red, the city shades", he states. His own city is a gorgeous spreading of feelings and emotion. "My favorite districts? Marais, with its exquisite place des Vosges.

Here, like in many other districts, you feel like in a village surrounded by people you are familiar with; the 18th arrondissement, in its popular and fun-loving aspect; the Latin district with rue Mazarine, rue de l'Ancienne Comédie and rue de Buci, with all its history and gastronomy. For instance, Le Procope: the first true Parisian café, is in rue de l'Ancienne Comédie and shields all the French cafés and brasserie history. Also the catacomb is an incredible underground world to discover, La Defence and its square for the wonderful view of the city center. Above all, I almost love everything of Paris, as I love Paris", he leaves, with an open hearted declaration of love for his city, like the winning ingredients of his pastry chef art.

**La Défense**
In 1976 the Catalan sculptor Joan Miró carried out the work "Two Fantastic Characters" at the Esplanade de la Dèfense.

# HÉLÈNE DARROZE

## A Culinary Delight Enthusiast

She believes gastronomy is a chance to get pleasure. Her dishes win, bewitch more than Paris does, for their aesthetic beauty and liveliness; they can raise emotions and mirror her mood. Ingredients are fundamental, she thinks.

And she respects their origin, season, freshness as if they were faithful friends to rely on. Chef Hélène Darroze admits any single detail of her creation reflects herself, is inspired by a smell, a memory, a taste, a color, a feeling. She admits that at this stage she can't make it without Paris. She's deeply attached to it... - "I've a symbiotic relationship with Paris, since I lived in London many years and I got back to Paris last year. Currently I can't think of any other place where to live. I have the opportunity to travel a lot, but I am always happy when I'm back", she states fervently. Her enthusiasm is contagious. She was titled the Veuve Clicquot best chef of the world, in 2015.

She jokes, describing Paris lively air. "What I love best and mostly dislike of Paris? Its accessible elegance and sophistication, best. Its snobbish air, worst", she says.

The secret of being a good restaurant owner is to be yourself, authentic, without following trends.

She was born in Villeneuve de Marsan, on 23rd February 1967, and she has always had culinary art in her blood. She's a fourth generation chef, her family has been running a restaurant in her birthplace for a long time.

She's proud of her origins, she comes from the South-West of France that she thinks stretches from Charenter to the Spanish area of the Basque country, including Périgord, Toulouse and reaching the Languedoc border section. It's a real cradle of culinary pleasure and cooking, as well as of a taste for enjoying the good life.

Before becoming a professional cook, Hélène wanted to study economics at the prestigious Ecole Supérieure de Commerce de Bordeaux to explore new fields. It's incredible how her first memories date back to what would become her destiny... "My first memory of the city is the dinner at the 'Tour D'Argent', a mythical restaurant of Paris. My mother invited me there to celebrate my eighteen birthday. This place provides a view of the Seine, Notre-Dame Cathedral and the Île de la Cité", she reminds, going back in time.

Restaurant Hélène Darroze

RUE D'ASSAS — PARIS

"My favorite district is Saint-Germain-des-Prés,
a small Parisian village, a borough of intellectuals,
artists and booksellers."

Place de Furstenberg is one of the most elegant squares in Paris.

After university, Hélène went to work at the great chef Alain Ducasse's office, in his restaurant Le Louis XV of Munich. He persuaded her to start working in his kitchen after three years of cooperation... It was the first time she cooked in a new environment. Before then, she had always worked in her family place. Once back in her homeland she kept working with them for a while and then at the Relais & Châteaux in Villeneuve-de-Marsan as her father asked her to run it. She opened her own restaurant Hélène Darroze in Paris in 1999, in the heart of Saint-Germain-des-Prés, in 4 rue d'Assas. Here she gained her first Michelin star, in 2001. Others followed...

Now she owns three restaurants. Apart from Paris, she runs restaurants in London at The Connaught Hotel and in Moscow. They made her successful and gain sympathy. Up to the point that, in 2007, she inspired Colette character in the Pixar animated film "Ratatouille".

The Ami Louis bistro, a well known restaurant among cinema celebrities and politician, is in **rue du Vertbois**, in the 3rd arrondissement.

The **Canal Saint-Martin**. Its banks are well appreciated by the Parisians for walks.

In 2012 she was admitted in the French Legion of Honor, as President Nicolas Sarcozy's Knight. "The secret of been a good restaurant owner is to be yourself, authentic, without following trends and fashions. To listen to your heart" she thinks speaking of her success. "I'll tell you a secret: when I got in Paris a great French chef told me that my cuisine wasn't enough 'Parisian' I didn't listen to him, I followed my heart and my instinct. And it worked", she states.

Hélène seems to enjoy her city conviviality every moment. Just like a gourmet able to make all dishes. "My favorite district is Saint-Germain-des-Prés, a small Parisian village, a borough of intellectuals, artists and booksellers. It's full of life, colors and soul. The Jardin du Luxembourg is here. The most beautiful garden in town. It's my district, as well, since I live here and know it perfectly well" she says.

Aroused by the peculiar curiosity featuring her culinary art and her lifestyle, she ventures and explores places bewitching her. "My favorite places are then Montmartre with the Basilica of the Sacre Coeur overlooking Paris, the exquisite place Furstenberg and place Dauphine, real islands of peace, the Canal Saint-Martin, the Cafè de Flore, a true city institution, the intellectuals and artists' café, the Ami Louis restaurant, the Comptoir de Camdeborde, the bakery, boulangerie, Poilane." This one, at 8 rue du Cherche-Midi, is truly appealing and boasts the best bread in the world... The Ami Louis, at

> "I have a symbiotic relationship with Paris...
> I have the opportunity to travel a lot,
> but I'm always happy when I'm back."

32 rue du Vertbois, is known as the most famous and characteristic bistro. It has few tables within a typically French atmosphere. It's based on traditional dishes, like lamb and foie gras. Among its customers: Francis Ford Coppola, Alice Waters, Bill Clinton and Jacques Chirac.

Le Comptoir de Camdeborde, 9 Carrefour de l'Odéon, is another suggestive bistro serving excellent fish and meat. Canal Saint-Martin area is also very interesting. It develops along the same name canal, with several shops. Some are even new local designers'. Cafés and bars are wrapped in a really magic, as well as attractive and romantic atmosphere. And you can also enjoy colorful graffiti on the walls.

Hélène is enthralled by Paris, both as a chef and personally, with all the suggestions you can discover along its roads, in its squares, its places, in the air... "Any food that reminds me of Paris? The jambon beurre sandwich, the baguette, bread, butter and ham sandwich. It's crunchy, sweet, tasty and owns its own personality", she

admits. "If I think about a smell for this city, it's definitely roasted chicken, when you pass by a Parisian butchery", she adds straight away. Then she reveals her romantic and dreamy side, as she reveals in her cuisine. "When I wonder about a color for this extraordinary metropolis, blue comes to my mind, as Paris is never as beautiful as under the blue sky reflecting in the Seine and in the chestnut leaves" she evokes, describing how wonderful and unforgettable some Parisian moments can be. Moments able to impress the mind as eternal memory traces.

Her picture doesn't end here but develops towards new happiness. Still culinary. "In the future? I' like to open a bistro in Paris. One that talks about my gastronomy, my roots, my South-West culinary heritage, since I'm made of tradition... why not a Grandma's cooking bistro? After all, I've written a book on Grandmas' recipes!", she ends, choosing Paris again and again as the destination of her experiments. She's authentic and unique like her Paris.

Le **Comptoir du Relais**. The chef Yves Camdeborde, an exponent of the so-called "bistronomie", has run the bistro in Saint-Germain-des-Prés. since 2005.

"My favorite places
are Montmartre,
with the Basilica
of the Sacre Coeur
overlooking Paris."

**Montmartre**
Montmartre magic atmosphere appeals to all tourists with the Basilica of
the Sacre Coeur overlooking the alleys.

# JEAN-LOUIS DEBRÉ
## The Politician and the Strategist

A man is made of his own ideas and thoughts. If he owns a big picture, he's able to conquer all of humankind and to mark history. An artist mainly tends to creativity, whereas a politician loves strategy, leading him to pursue his promises and his ideal. The latter must go beyond political disposition and serve the community best to search for a better world. Jean-Louis Debré is doubtlessly a political figure and a magistrate who marked the destiny of Paris – a city he loves deeply – and of France. "I love Paris, not only for its radiant history, but also because of its respect for tradition, for the past melting with a search for modernity. Paris is a city where culture arises from the alliance of past, present and future", he says as charming as a man of culture can be.

After all, Debré comes from a respectful and ancient traditional family, boasting important characters within the political, scientific and artistic fields. He was born on 30th September 1944 in Toulouse. His twin brother Bernard is a politician as well.

Their father is former Prime Minister Michel. On his father's side, he's the grandson of the well known pediatrician Robert, whereas his uncle was the painter Olivier. On her mother's side, his grandfather was the architect Charles Lemaresquier, while among his ancestors: Chief Rabbi Simon Debré, from Westhoffen, in Alsace.

Jean-Louis graduated in Law, has a qualification in Public Law and Political Science and achieved a PhD in Public Law, with a dissertation on "General De Gaulle's constitutional ideas". During his education, he also attended the Institut d'études Politiques de Paris and the École Nationale de la Magistrature, getting fascinated by the French capital, full of political and social, as well as intellectual, cultural and artistic hints. When he became a magistrate, he started dealing with organized crime, gangsterism and even terrorism.

In 1989 he decided he wanted to enter politics. He had already carried out several activity in the field and had gained experience. He was elected Deputy of the Assemblée Nationale for the RPR (Rally for the Republic) and was re-elected in the following legislatures. He was also the assistant of Jean Tiberi (Paris mayor between 1995 and 2001). As the Minister of Home Affairs under Alain Juppé's government, between 1995 and 1997, he was the President of the RPR group at the Assemblée Nationale from 1997 to 2002 when it was annected to the UMP (Union for a Popular Movement).

> Paris is a city where culture arises from the alliance of past, present and future.

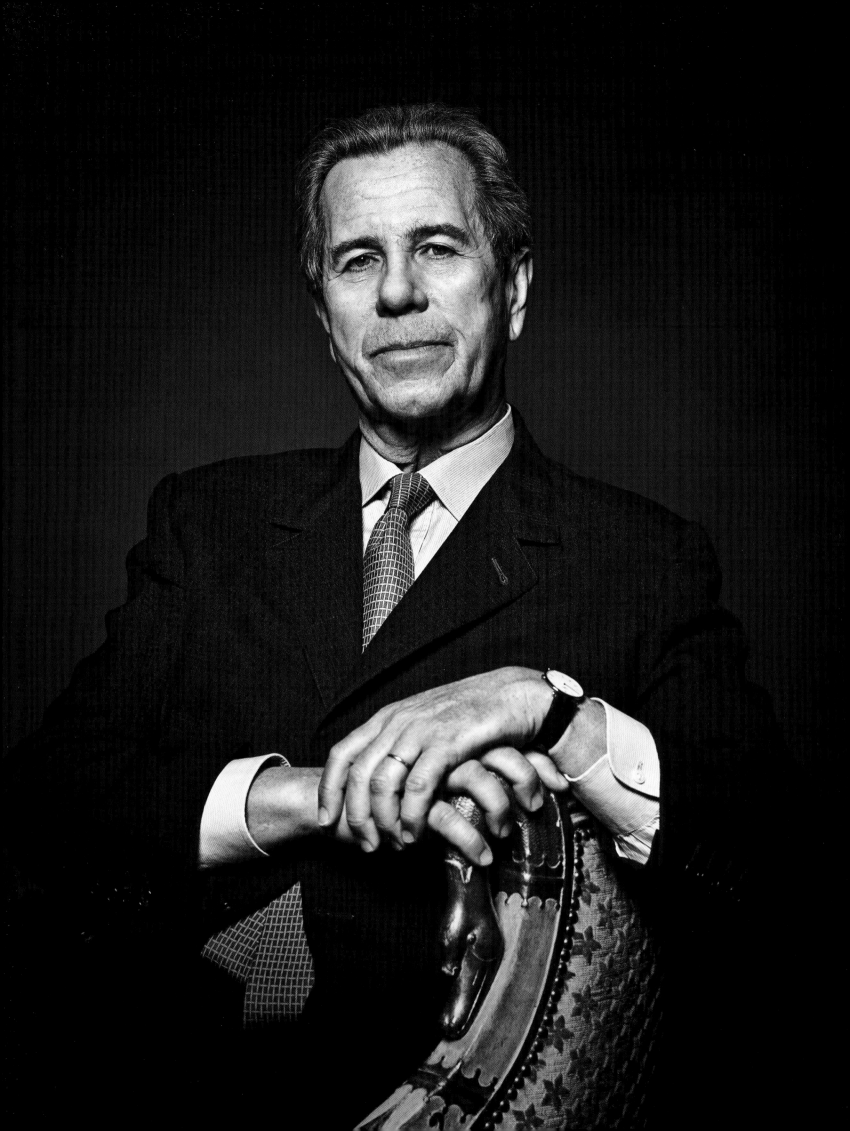

In the same year he became the President of the Assemblée Nationale in charge until 2007. He was very close to former President of the Republic Jacques Chirac. They established a long-term and trusty collaboration (Debré became Chirac's technical consultant in 1973). He stood out, choosing a consensual style and a great respect for the opposition. In 2007 he was appointed President of the Constitutional Council by Chirac and had been in charge until 5th March 2016. Currently he's the President of the Superior Council on Archives. During his career, Debré has published many books. He's passionate about writing and deepened some issues, like justice and politics which he's fond of.

Jean-Louis Debré is enchanted by his Paris, as much as by the causes he cares about deeply. He finds it difficult to pick out a favorite district of the city, for example: "How not to be seduced by the atmosphere of the several districts? Each one owns its own soul, its own identity. You need to watch, observe, take your time", he argues. Then, thinking of the monuments and places he gets inspired by, or simply, touch his heart, he starts describing: "You can't help but getting fascinated by the city center, from the 1st to the 2nd arrondissement. The Palais-Royal, the Louvre, the Galerie Vivienne and the Galerie Colbert, the Passage Choiseul, the Passage des Princes, or the Galerie Véro-Dodat, the Comédie-Française, the Théâtre du Palais-Royal, the Monarchy and Republic memories, Molière, Colette and many other well known characters", he says recalling literary and cultural thoughts that have excited him during his long-lasting relationship with the city.

**The Palais-Royal**
The metal spheres decorate the Belgian artist Pol Bury's fountains in the Cour d'Orléans of the Palais-Royal and reflect the historic building architecture.

In particular, he admits his favorite place in Paris is the Palais-Royal, classified as a French historical monument since 1994, a real historic icon. Placed opposite the museum Louvre, northern side, it hosts the Council of State and the Constitutional Council, together with the Salle Richelieu, the Comédie-Française's theater. In 1986, Daniel Buren's work "Deux Plateaux" was installed in the main yard of the Palais-Royal. The building history, like a magic tale, is lost in the mists of time. The Palace was built on Cardinal Richelieu's request, as his own personal residency in Paris, by architect Jacques Lemercier who completed his work in 1639. After Richelieu's death, in 1642, it became a Royal residency and that's when it got its current name. Many noble dynasties lived here. Among them, the Orleans and Philippe d'Orleans, King Louis XIV's younger brother, who reckoned the palace too small for his entire court and decided to move to the Louvre, first, and then to Versailles. With Philippe and his wife, Duchess Anne Henrietta, the Palais-Royal reached its peak, adorned with splendid ornamental gardens and the hall of pompous dances. Since then, the Palais-Royal has always had a key role in Paris and France history. Watching it today, in all its glory, one can't help thinking of its important past and the events it witnessed.

The **Galerie Vivienne**, in the 2nd arrondissement, was inaugurated in 1826 and has been a historical monument since 1974. It's decorated in a Neoclassical style with mosaic floors.

The glass dome on top of the **Galerie Colbert** rotunda throws the light on the statue of Eurydice Bitten by the Snake, by Nanteuil. The Galerie is part of France cultural heritage.

Debré underlines how history is hidden in every corner of such a beautiful city and he admits that all Paris bewitches him. "It's important not to be locked up in just one district of Paris...

Paris popular **flea markets** are full of collectibles.

"I love Paris, not only for its radiant history,
but also because of its respect for tradition,
for the past melting with a search for modernity."

You are just enchanted by the Hotel de Ville, Place des Vosges, the Pantheon, the Palais Garnier. How not to enjoy walking along the Seine or the markets, like the Batignolles, the Raspail, the Aligre ones or the Enfants Rouges one in Marais?", he points out. "I like other places, as well: I love visiting the Palais Bourbon and the nearby Hotel de Lassay, wandering around the Musée Rodin, admiring the court of the des Invalides Hotel, breathing Montmartre or Buttes-Chaumont park", he wishes to add.

Thinking about the changes that his city has occurred over time, he states: "Paris evolves, that's understandable and some buildings question me, especially the Defense district, as it provides a surprising view, from place de la Concorde to the Arc de Triomphe up to the sky...", he says, arousing a certain, unexpected curiosity.
Thinking of a color representing Paris, Debré states: "Blue, like the sky, optimism, hope, and, of course, France...", stating a deep love for his country, deeply connected with his city: France's beating heart.

The **Institut de France** and the Hotel des Invalides domes.

# INÈS DE LA FRESSANGE
## The Parisian

Some women leave their mark. You can't help noticing it when you observe them. A glance is enough... The rustling of a skirt kindly caressing her knees... A red belt tightening a jacket tied on a blouse. A sleeveless black dress with a pair of big sun-glasses, like the old-time divas' ones. A very light beige raincoat sliding over like a second skin when you climb up a staircase. Inès de la Fressange is all this and much more: the true icon of Paris style. The elegance of this extraordinary city reflects on herself like a beautiful and magic mirror. She is considered as a symbol of the city itself, like one of its monuments. The real Parisian.

"You don't have to be born in Paris to own a Parisian stile. Paris style is an attitude, a state of the mind",

> You don't have to be born in Paris to own a Parisian stile. Paris style is an attitude, a state of the mind.

says Inès to outline the real Parisian DNA, restating a concept already expressed in her guide "The Parisian. A Guide to Chic", written together with the fashion journalist Sophie Gachet: less is more. It teaches you how to get dressed like a Parisian on the basis of a collection of clothes combining seven affordable items of clothing to match with fashion accessories.

Fashion is pure fun for her, a kind of "dolce vita" developing in its constant and intensive relationship with Paris. She breathes the "air du temps", she states, and then decides what to wear, always in her own exclusive way. A uniqueness tying herself to this metropolis, the capital of dressing well par excellence. Inès aims at standing out, distinguishing, relying on an extreme attention to detail though based on simplicity. Personality really matters, practicality is worth more than expensive and unwearable clothes. And that's how a trend is born.

"My relationship with this place? I've always loved fashion and Paris is the city of fashion, with no doubt", she says. She was born on 11th August 1957 in Gassin, Var, from André de Seignard, Marquise de La Fressange, a broker, and Cecilia 'Lita' Sánchez-Cirez, an Argentinian model. Inès grew up in a 18th century residence in Paris, together with her two brothers, Emmanuel and Yvan. Her paternal grandmother was Simone Lazard, heiress of the bankers Lazard dynasty. Her aristocratic roots will come to light in her very sophisticated, almost minimalist, always classy style. But Inès wins with her congeniality and spontaneity, with her always being, naturally, herself. After all, just like Paris, she's authentic in her beauty which knows no bounds, like time passing. And in her fondness of fashion, Inès gets inspired by the glimpses of the districts.

Meanwhile she is a model, the city itself and the Parisians look up to her.

She wonders why so many tourists only favor the Champs-Elysées and Rue de Rivoli, instead of entering in districts she defines as more interesting and intriguing, like for example the 11th arrondissement on Rive Droite, currently in full Renaissance.

Inès cooperated with great brands in Paris. In 1980 she signed an exclusive contract with the fashion house Chanel and became Karl Lagerfeld's muse. Despite some differences of opinion, he has always considered her extraordinary. Their partnership probably broke when in 1989 Inès decided to lend her image to the Marienne, the embodiment of the French Republic. According to Lagerfeld, the Marienne was a provincialism symbol and clearly stated that he didn't want to dress monuments up. However, Inès, kept catwalking, slightly zigging and zagging, as she did in a

**24 rue de Grenelle**
Opened in 2015 in the 7th arrondissement, Inès de la Fressange's boutique offers a "posh" wide range of products.

Good taste, elegance and Parisian spirit make Inès de la Fressange's boutique a destination
to jot down on notebooks by all those who are looking for **"quincaillerie chic"**.

> "I've always loved fashion and Paris
> is the city of fashion."

venue for Jean-Paul Gaultier who she cooperated with as a designer and consultant. And she was on Chanel stage for the Spring-Summer collection in 2011, whereas Diego della Valle wanted her as Roger Vivier's ambassador.

"What about the relationship between Paris and fashion? It's difficult to explain in a nutshell, but here it happens for sure! Actually it's the so-called Pantheon style: it's a mood, a spirit and special style gaining success all over the world!", she says, referring to that creative juices and sparkling flair marking the French metropolis in her eyes. According to Inès, Paris is indeed the birthplace of style, but first and foremost it is the birthplace of love. Always very passionate, both in her personal and public life, she has always followed her heart. So, in 1990, in Tarascona, France, she married the entrepreneur Luigi d'Urso, a Neapolitan, a books and art lover, of aristocratic origin like her. In 2006, Luigi died of a heart attack, leaving a shadow upon her existence. Their two daughters, Nine-Marie and Violette-Marie, respectively born in 1994 and 1999, gave great joy and unforgettable memories to their parents. Today they are both very fond of their father's Neapolitan origins and therefore they feel themselves Italian as well, despite being really attached to Paris.

What strikes Inès about today Paris? She loves traveling and getting in touch with worldwide cultures, but she keeps being bewitched by the variety that this extraordinary city shields among its roads and its districts. They are all different, they all have their own personality, but are indissolubly linked together, like a big puzzle that doesn't work if you miss even just one piece. "Paris is like many different cities in one and gathers together different times and enchanting places all in one magic universe", she argues.

Obviously, even in the most absolute example of perfection there are some flaws... "If I have to work out something I don't like about Paris... Well, maybe there are never enough new places?", she wonders, even though in the end she isn't even so sure about it.

Moreover, Inès knows well the most beautiful spots of her city, up to the point of having written two guides about not to miss places. "Some addresses keep repeating in my mind, as they are the ones I call 'not to be missed', unique among their kind: Soeur, Marie-Hélène de Taillac, Le Bon Saint-Pourçain, Adelline...", she confesses. She describes them, among others, in her guide "My Paris". Soeur, in rue Bonaparte is a really exclusive boutique gathering together "too much teenager clothes". Marie-Hélène de Taillac, in rue de Tournon, is a small place, a real bijoux that sells Indian style jewelry "that will make you happy". Adeline, in rue Jacob, has a unique style and "very simple jewelry". Le Bon Saint-Pourçain in rue Servandoni, is a typical space with a suggestive atmosphere, so popular to be often crowded. Inès confesses that it has always been her favorite restaurant, the one she finds truly Parisian and capable of revealing the spirit of the capital. She recommends ordering the well known vinaigrette leeks, poultry, always well prepared, and the dark chocolate mousse she calls "unforgettable".

Reflections in the shop window of **Marie-Hélène de Taillac**'s boutique in rue de Tournon.

**Place Vendôme**, the symbol of Parisian elegance.
The **Ville Lumière**: The Austerlitz column overlooks place Vendôme and the city lights.

Among Inès' favorite places, some are very well known, though iconic, like the Café de Flore, in boulevard Saint-Germain, and the restaurant Les Parigots, in rue du Château-d'Eau. She admits she has nothing against clichés, provided that they are really up to. Besides, she loves the Paris of Amélie Poulain, the protagonist of the movie Amélie, starring the actress Audrey Tautou.

Since Autumn 2015, Inès has had her own destination in Paris. Inès de la Fressange, number 24 rue de Grenelle, on the Rive Gauche. A boutique entirely reflecting her tastes, together with her brand. She sells both first-hand designed products, like the clothes she makes in a glass wall laboratory, and the creations of friends and designers she meets in her journeys around the world. She herself describes her boutique as a kind of "grocery-household products, where to buy both an elegant leather bag and a tooth-brush holder". Here you can find fashion items, shoes, accessories, jewelry, toys, sun-glasses, gift and fancy goods and home furniture. One of the most original pieces? A pink rubber bambi serving as a liquid soap dispenser... But everything evolves and renews itself. Who can predict how long it will still be there, considering the popularity of the place? And both in its interior design and in the choice of products, the whole shop is a blooming of a happy, lively, sparkling and funny spirit, like the real Parisian's one.

What is it that keeps her involved in this city? "Paris inspires me, since history and beauty are everywhere here, but first and foremost it offers you a beautiful life in touch with many people of several cultures", she underlines. And she ponders: "If I have to think about a color defining Paris that's navy blue: like the sky at night, uniforms, a part of the flag. And also because it's my favorite color!"

# CHRISTIAN DE PORTZAMPARC

## The Quick-Change Artist

He's in pursuit of shapes and meanings. Of world figures, of time figures. Of lyricism featured by buildings diversity. Of "towers", skyscrapers aiming at a vertical line, with sculpture-like dimensions, crystallized in prismatic characteristics. His buildings often become landmarks gathering an area to create a connection pole, or attraction poles, with a wide urban surroundings landscape. Christian de Portzamparc, a well known architect and city planner, painter and visionary, shapes up spaces where the interior and the exterior melt together and work as catalysts for the dynamics of the city itself. Since the 80s, his intense passion for music has led him to carry out works on track with it or with dance. He reached all the corners of the world with his arts. He carried his vision all over the place but its heart beats in Paris.

"My relationship with Paris? I'm so used to this city, that it is hard to say... Above all, when I'm back from a journey in Africa or in Asia, I am struck by Paris authenticity, which I never stop discovering again and again", he tells, pausing to gather his thoughts. "You can tell Paris uniqueness is appreciated all over the world. You can spot it for example when you walk along the Seine, in wide green areas and in its beautiful gardens. The homogeneous wisdom of Paris could also bore you. Paris is very wise, very chic, maybe too much. When I step into this metropolis, I repeat it's marvelous, really magic and special, though. But I got too used to it, and that's my fault. I think that's very common. Paris has its own architecture, its own dimensions, connected and renewed throughout centuries. And the space variety is wonderful here", he carries on.

De Portzamparc was born in Casablanca (Morocco) on 5th May 1944. He spent his teenage in Rennes and studied at the École Nationale Supérieure des Beaux-arts in Paris. He graduated in 1969. He acknowledges that the city has inspired his creative vein right from the start. "When I was a young student, I used to spend entire hours at the museum of Modern Art or the Impressionists museum, beyond Les Tuileries towards Les Halles: I love the Musée d'Orsay and the Centre Pompidou, of course", he argues.

At first, Christian approached architecture, inspired by some of Le Corbusier's sketches, but then he withdrew almost immediately from studying modern architecture, getting aware of the fact that in Paris you can't completely destroy the past. "During my studies,

> Today I would say that Paris is like a metaphysical calendar defining itself and growing up in time.

The **Grand Palais** and the **Petit Palais**, in Art Nouveau style, were built for the Universal Exhibition in 1900.

I got very interested in modernist architecture. I used to love Le Corbusier and Ludwig Mies van der Rohe's works. Then gradually I realized that wanting to erase Paris authentic identity was a mistake. That would never be possible. Therefore I addressed to the small neighboring towns. They didn't ask for renewing or modernizing. We are encountering big changes and the modernization of Paris outskirts, mostly thanks to the Grand Paris project. Unfortunately, we often face conservative associations, impervious to changes, trying to block everything", he explains referring to the limitation that can stop an artist's work and the problems a professional has to deal with.

In Paris he made several architecture masterpieces, like the popular residence of Hautes-Formes in 1979, in the 13th arrondissement. In the 80s he drew up the open block concept, *îlot ouvert*, in contrast with the two models shaping all the 19th century architecture:

**Alexander III bridge** was inaugurated on the occasion of the Universal Exhibition and it was the first bay bridge crossing the Seine.

Haussmann's block and Le Corbusier's block. Among his works in Paris: the Musée Bourdelle enlargement, the Cité de la Musique, the restoration of the Palais des Congrès, the Tour Granite for the Sociéte Générale La Défense, Le Monde headquarter.

His worldwide works are: l'École de Danse de l'Opéra National de Paris in Nanterre, the LVMH and One57 skyscrapers in New York, the Music City in Rio, the Philarmonie Luxembourg in Luxemburg.

"In 1995 he worked out a new Conservatory of the Cité de la Musique placed in the Villette, a park built in 1984-1985 and completed at the end of 1990", he underlines remembering one of his most famous works, before thinking about some less known projects... "I restored the Renaissance Hotel facade, at the Arc de Triomphe. It's made of a glass twine", he works out. "Then I created the Galeo building, the builder and real estate businessman Bouygues' s Registered Office. A concrete red fiber building and a glass scales one. It's placed at the gates of Paris, in Issy les-Moulineaux, near the Boulevard périphérique."

**The Observatoire Fountain**
Emmanuel Frémiet sculpted the horses decorating the fountain which was carried out by Jean-Baptiste Carpeaux for the Jardin Marco Polo in 1874.

"You can tell Paris uniqueness is appreciated all over the world.
You can spot it for example when you walk along the Seine,
in wide green areas and in its beautiful gardens."

The **Palais du Luxembourg**, currently the Senate house, was initially built in the 17th century by
the architect Salomon de Brosse as Maria de' Medici's residence (Louis XIII's mother).

He was awarded many recognitions appointing him a worldwide icon over the years. He was the first chair in "artistic creation" at the Collège de la France and in 1989 he was titled Commandeur des Arts et des Lettres by the Minister of Culture. Among the many prizes won, in 1990 he was awarded the Grand Prix d'Architecture of the Ville de Paris, given by Paris municipality. In 1992 the Acadèmie Francaise d'Architecture conferred him a medal for the École de Danse de l'Opéra National de Paris and for the Cité de la Musique; in 1994 he received the Pritzker, a kind of architecture Nobel prize and in 2004 he won the Grand Prix de l'Urbanisme. In 1995, he was titled École Spéciale d'Architecture headmaster, in Paris. Here he deepened his passion for teaching with the wish for conveying his art to many other young talents.

His study in Paris, the Atelier Christian de Portzamparc is constantly researching, experimenting and working out concepts and ideas to put in practice, a sort of "urban laboratory". In 2006 he gathered all his work and masterpieces in a big book telling his artistic life and production. He's passionate about challenges leading him to mark history with quick-change works, featuring him. "I worked out a new district along the Seine, called Massena where I experimented my 'open blocks'. This is a particularly interesting project. It's a very lively area with its University, offices, many boutiques and a park.

**La Défense**
Chirstian de Portzamparc is active in the Défense district with his projects contributing to renovate the city skyline.

The **Centre Georges Pompidou** external staircase, planned by Piano & Rogers studio in 1977.

"Paris is very wise,
very chic,
maybe too much."

**Stravinsky Fountain**, by Jean Tinguely e Niki de Saint Phalle, is near the Centre Pompidou and is inspired by the Russian composer's works.

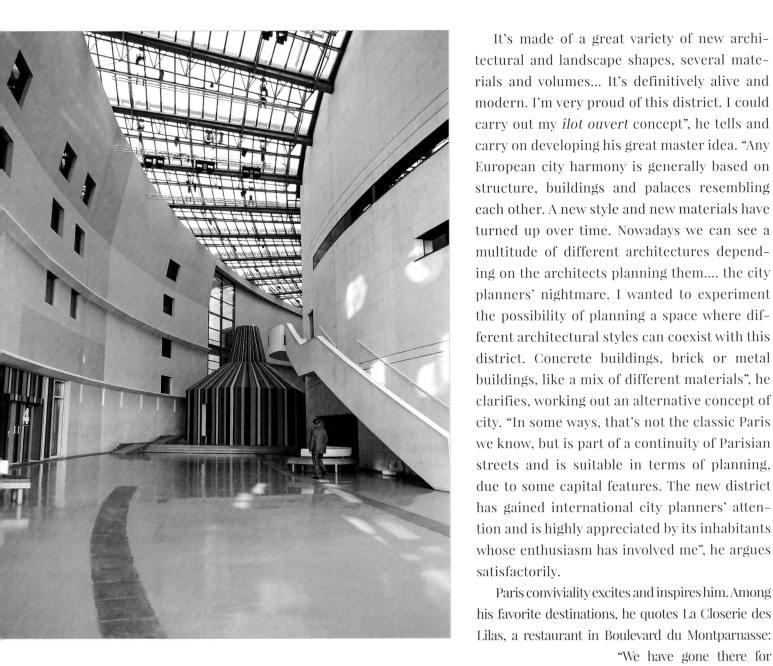

It's made of a great variety of new architectural and landscape shapes, several materials and volumes... It's definitively alive and modern. I'm very proud of this district. I could carry out my *îlot ouvert* concept", he tells and carry on developing his great master idea. "Any European city harmony is generally based on structure, buildings and palaces resembling each other. A new style and new materials have turned up over time. Nowadays we can see a multitude of different architectures depending on the architects planning them.... the city planners' nightmare. I wanted to experiment the possibility of planning a space where different architectural styles can coexist with this district. Concrete buildings, brick or metal buildings, like a mix of different materials", he clarifies, working out an alternative concept of city. "In some ways, that's not the classic Paris we know, but is part of a continuity of Parisian streets and is suitable in terms of planning, due to some capital features. The new district has gained international city planners' attention and is highly appreciated by its inhabitants whose enthusiasm has involved me", he argues satisfactorily.

Paris conviviality excites and inspires him. Among his favorite destinations, he quotes La Closerie des Lilas, a restaurant in Boulevard du Montparnasse:

**The Musée de la Musique**
The museum is part of the Cité de la Musique and hosts an important collection of musical instruments dating back to 15th-20th centuries.

The **Cité de la Musique** was inaugurated in 1995 and conceived by de Portzamparc. It's placed on La Villette park and currently cooperates with Jean Nouvel Philarmonie.

"We have gone there for ages with my wife Elisabeth. This place has inevitably changed over the years, but we keep going there. In the end it keeps its intimate atmosphere and they serve very good food.

The southern facade of **Le Monde** office, planned by de Portzamparc,
is covered with huge glass panels envisaging the idea of a newspaper page.

This evolution across time can be found in the streets and roads of the district Batignolles, a popular and lively district keeping a sort of authenticity", he admits. "As in all the cities I visit, I love discovering just opened places, new museums or bookshops. They are so many in Paris, they all have a peculiar and vibrant style! I love it!", he explains, showing how his own city is still able to surprise and amuse him.

His eyes are drawn to details as well as to the stone and material nuances composing the French capital buildings.

"When I think about a color for Paris, I think of dark gray. If you look at it carefully, you real-ize it is made up of a very few colors", he says.

Christian de Portzamparc has a particular vision of the French metropolis. It keeps its charm intact, despite passing time and it really doesn't seem to get old in a continuous renewal process: "Today I would say that Paris is like a metaphysical calendar defining itself and growing up in time", he concludes. "Paris is a city full of history, leaving a trail and being part of its inhabitants memory. But that doesn't mean we should keep it like a museum. It has to adapt itself to time and changes, adding some features of modernity.

**The îlot ouvert**
North Massena redevelopment project, coordinated by de Portzamparc, recalls the "open block" concept.

# ELLIOTT ERWITT
## The Great Master of Photography

His art is the mirror of humanity itself, with all its shades and facets; it's rich in penetrating irony, like in a sort of human *commedia dell'arte*. An endless tale of souls, caught in a fleeting moment or overwhelmed by it; of people engaged in some activities or in the exclusiveness of life, portrayed in their daily life emotions. Love, pleasure, fun, the grotesque, commitment, playing, work, intimacy, pills of tenderness... And then an amazing series of dogs, spot behind a tree, at people's feet, in a café, in a car, in human gestures, full of sensitivity and feelings, immortalized in spending their four legged daily life. Elliot Erwitt is one of the greatest photography masters, an artist of exclusive shots, identifiable in his unique style, almost black and white. He marked history and left traces of unforgettable memory. He got inspired by Charlie Chaplin in his artistic production, skilful in "switching between laughing and crying", being able to make people smile, always in search for the perfect shot...

"I made a book, entirely devoted to Paris, and it expresses all my love for the city: you can look at all the times I enjoyed my city best", he admits. His Paris takes shape and turns into photos as if they were a bolt from the blue: a guy walking arming around his girl-friend along the Champs-Élysées with his hand nonchalantly lying on her bottom; the silhouette of a man hopping under his opened umbrella in a rainy day at the Trocadero. He passes by a couple crouching under their umbrella thorn by the Parisian wind. Beautiful women., gleaming out of nowhere. One is wearing a full-feathered hat, reading *Vogue* opposite the Café de Flore. One is hopping along the Seine in heeled shoes. Another one is watching herself in the mirror, tightening her lips as if she was making up... At times, you can spot portraits of well known people, in their own private life, like Isabelle Huppert with her dog and a bed full of teddy bears and puppets, or the amazing Sophia Loren while shooting a film in Paris. A not too serious Simone de Beauvois, Josef Koudelka taking pictures, Marcel Marceau at the theater. But Erwitt is mostly enchanted by passers-by, waiters, museum visitors and his dear dogs.

Although he does not live in Paris, Erwitt speaks like a true Parisian: "I was born in Paris, but I just left when I was two months old. I don't have childhood memories, but I remember when I came back after the War. When I was in the Army, between 1951 and 1953, I used to live near Paris and I would visit it often.

> Paris remains a beautiful city thanks to its incredible and incomparable beauty.

In 1989, Erwitt took this picture which encloses Paris essence for the **Eiffel Tower centennial.**

I'm very familiar with Paris, since I have been on business here – all year long, working out projects and publicity campaigns for the French tourism board", he says.

He was born in Paris, in 1928 from Jewish and Russian parents. He spent his childhood in Italy, before moving back to France, when he was ten, and to the United States, in 1939. They settled in New York for a couple of years, then they moved to Los Angeles, where Erwitt developed an attitude for photography, experimenting in the darkrooms of Hollywood High School and of Los Angeles City College. Once back in New York in 1948, he learned the art of cinematography attending the New School for Social Research. In 1949, he started traveling around France and Italy, with a Rolleiflex camera and in 1951, he was in the Army in France and Germany working as a photographer assistant and as a senior photographer.

**Everlasting**
In 1909, the Eiffel Tower was about to be demolished, but it was saved and made useful as a basis for communication antennae: currently is France's landmark.

**Dogs and kids** are Erwitt's favorite subjects.
The great photographer has never given up his sense of humor in portraying them.

Then he chose New York as his headquarter, despite owning a vague concept of residence, as he points out: "You are in a specific place at a specific time, since you're not going anywhere else." In New York he met several photographers like Edward Steichen, Robert Capa who would become his mentor, and Roy Stryker who would charge him with many projects, such as shooting Pittsburgh. In 1953 he became a member of the Magnum Photos agency and started taking magazine and reportage photos, as well as working out artistic, publicity and commercial projects. In 1968 he was appointed President of the Magnum agency which gathered the best photographers. "As for the many artists in Paris, I can't help but thinking about my colleagues, Magnum Photos' photographers. One of my dearest friend, unfortunately passed away, was Henri Cartier-Bresson. I didn't use to surround myself with highly famous artists, but I've always been close to my colleagues. We own a study at place de Clichy and we usually meet there or nearby. When we were younger, we used to stay in Saint-Germain-des-Prés. We've moved around the city over the years. Our very first office was on the right side in Saint Philippe du Roule. It was in 1947, my very creative time, though we weren't grown-up by then", he remembers, letting his thoughts flow back in time. "I regularly come back to Paris in November for the Paris Photo exhibition and I like spending time with colleagues and friends. It's a really pleasant and positive time, it also evokes nice memories."

he says, as a group photo proves. It was shot with all Magnum's photographers in funny poses in Paris, in 1988.

During the 70s, Erwitt produced several documentaries and in the 80s he shot TV satirical comedies and some films among them, "Arthur Penn: the Director" (1970), "Beauty Knows No Pain" (1971), "Red, White and Bluegrass" (1973) e "The Glass Makers of Herat" (1997). He kept working a lot as a photographer though, and proclaimed himself "King" of fine arts. His photos were displayed in art galleries and in the most prestigious world museums. He also worked out many volumes of photographs on Rome, New York and Paris, as well as dog publications. Moreover, he organized several photo exhibitions, like the Modern Art Museum one in Paris (Palais de Tokyo).

Paris is one of his favorite topics. He can't define it in just one shot: "I find it difficult to choose my favorite picture of Paris. I've shot this city for more than seventeen years. I guess the pictures inside my book 'Paris' are all beautiful, as they represent what I love best of Paris, as a street photographer", he points out.

He tells his relationship with the French capital, with the same intensity. He's not just a common visitor. "My relationship with Paris? Beauty and fondness, for sure", he states, adding: "I don't see Paris as a tourist any longer and I don't find it so different from other cities I travel to: I mean it's no sur-

**Parisian Dogs**
Erwitt is particularly interested in shooting the relationship between dogs and human beings. His great ability to catch the moment does the rest.

> "I like shooting in the late afternoon or before sunset, the so called golden hour."

prise, I'm familiar with it. It may sound odd, but it happens with all the places I know well. In Paris I feel at home, I can even relate to the most bad-tempered Parisians", he admits with his typical irony. "I must confess Paris is a wonderful city, as everyone knows. The Parisians may be more complicated and it was difficult for them to cope with the terrorist attacks in 2015. At that time, the city didn't look as safe as it used to be. Despite this, Paris remains a beautiful city, able to make up for any complaint thanks to its incredible and incomparable beauty. It's so positive", he explains smiling.

His attention as a photographer stretches on every Parisian life moments: "I think shooting Paris can be interesting any time. It depends on what you want to catch. If you like to catch the external beauty of the city, then light is important. In this case I like shooting in the late afternoon or before sunset, the so called golden hour. If you take pictures of people or their activities, the time doesn't matter, but the subject. I've always found it important to tell sto-

The **Jardin des Tuileries** octagonal basin, towards place de la Concorde, is one of the best place to have a rest in the city center.

ries throughout my photography", he underlines talking about his artistic view. "I don't shoot 'on behalf of', any longer. That means I favor black and white, a more suitable style to the subjects and things I'm interested in. I don't find light as fundamental as other color-devoted photographers do. The subject comes first, as I said", he carries on revealing what enchants him most behind a camera. "I don't see landscapes particularly appealing, instead, human condition, people's activities, special attitudes, peculiarities, instant shots, provide your own personal view. Anyway, I worked with the French tourism board and caught colorful moments of Paris, with amazing people and city glimpses", he adds, conveying the several aspects of his profession.

Thinking about the season he likes best in Paris, he says: "As a photographer I've always favored Spring and Fall in Paris. Winter, despite being interesting in other respects, makes the city mournful as a cold Northern European city. In Spring you feel happy and it's a bloom of colors. The Parisians show their best", he confides. "As for Paris light, we should remember it's called the city of lights. There's a connection here. I prefer the longest days before Summer: it's the best time in Paris", he adds soon after.

**The Glass Pyramid**
Modern structure, ancient shape: the glass Pyramid in the Cour Napoleon represents the main entrance for the Louvre visitors.

"The Eiffel Tower is often in my photos,
it's a real icon, with its unique and imposing structure.
And as you can see, you immediately
understand you're in Paris."

The Eiffel Tower appears a lot in his photos, from a very personal point of view; lit by huge lights on top, in the mist, like a lighthouse in a stormy night in a Gothic tale. It reflects in the Seine, in the glassiness of a curtain tissue, a miniature in a dealer's hands, and a giant in a child's eyes; behind a bush, placed side by side to scaffolding...

"The Eiffel Towel is often in my photos, it's a real icon, with its unique and imposing structure. And as you can see, you immediately understand you're in Paris", he clearly explains.

He dwells on what has always fascinated him of Paris: its museums. In his shots you can rediscover the Louvre from a different point of view, throughout daily pictures, as if they were sketches of amused tourists watching paintings in a kind of irreverence. Or something unexpected comes, like the image of Napoleon's stuffed horse at the Hotel des Invalides, displaying some grotesque irony... "Paris is rich in history and museums. The Rodin Museum is my favorite, I find it unique. It's Rodin's home, his atelier, and has been totally renovated. I strongly recommend it. It's a museum you can visit and enjoy in one day, unlike more traditional museums taking ages to be visited", he suggests and wonders about another special place. "I also find The Guimet Museum very interesting. On Eastern art. It's exclusive and impressive as well. There are others, of course, like the Louvre or the Cen-

tre Pompidou, but they are more predictable", he adds, pondering the difference between the incomparably lively Parisian museums and the others. "In Paris, like in many other European cities, you can spend a lot of time in a museum. But here the government is a great sponsor, despite the budget having been reduced: and as for museums, we stay active to best show the city from a historical and artistic point of view", he points out.

Erwitt smiles when he remembers Douglas Sloan's documentary "Elliott Erwitt: I Bark at Dogs" where he tells the secret to best immortalize his favorite subjects: "to bark at dogs". Our four-footed friends are the main protagonists in Paris, as shown in his pictures: a dog jumping beside his owner's feet, another sitting at the restaurant or driving or in his owner's arms... there are those who are pulling on a leash, watching with their fur standing on end, walking proudly along a paved road, trying to socialize or playing with a kid, curling up on an old chair of a flea market, studying strategic approaches, barking or busy in other dog activities... "I portrayed dogs all over the world and in Paris, as well. I've always owned dogs in my life and I have a very special relationship with them. Dogs can enter restaurants in Paris, unlike in other countries or cities, as for example, the United States. French dogs are special, then... as many seem smaller than their standard, more careful and observer,

Known as the "esplanade of human rights", the **Trocadero** esplanade pays tribute to the Universal Declaration of Human Rights, signed at the nearby Palais de Chaillot in 1948.

more clever than other dogs in the world. I think they even bark French! If you have some kind of experience, you can figure it out. It's a very sharp and accurate barking, just like a Parisian dog can do. It owns even a sense of space, of its presence, like few dogs own. There is a slight difference among dogs in the world, like the Italian ones, the ones from Milan. If you own a particular attitude towards them, you can notice it. Trust me", he explains with enthusiasm and the magic sensitivity of an animal lover.

His Paris is portrayed with the same artistic intensity, in street life and in intimate shots like rooms, buildings, stations, shops or markets interiors. Portrays of people at work, performing at the circus or at the theater, busy in moving house, relaxing and meeting at a restaurant or at a café, strolling along roads full of posters and colors oozing even from black and white, in a park, at the metro or in a winter street among tree trunks, while kissing, having coffee naked in bed; some are models in unusual poses, others are quickly getting on a bike... Some other times, his photographer eye lies on details of windows, buildings or interiors, chairs, left adrift on the ground, children meetings, shadows, dark silhouette standing powerful in front of the lens. "Street life is very interesting in Paris. It's where many people socialize. And there's something irresistibly enchanting: the language. It's awesome. It's expressive, you can say many things in a few words. It's one of France

The Jardin Marco Polo hosts the **Fontaine de l'Observatoire** with bronze sculptures.
Also known as the Fontaine des Quatre-Parties-du-Monde.

and Paris main attractions, I think", he admits, revealing something that is normally hidden beyond his camera, but that you can figure out by looking at him. Erwitt pauses on other special sides of the city: "Parisian flats are pretty small and I think that's the reason why people enjoy socializing more in cafés, bars and restaurants than at home, as far as I'm concerned, at least. In Paris a lot takes place outdoors, in the street, in bars. That makes the city so lively, all year long."

Erwitt tells his personal Paris, providing pleasure as his photography does: "Paris has changed during the years and I long for old-time Paris. Cordiality has decreased, but it may grow even more in the future. And the awesomeness of the city, as I said, stays untouched. During the latest years, I have long been in Paris for work and I like reaching the South, the Provence from here. There you can breathe an authentic and fascinating atmosphere, like in the old-time Paris", he acknowledges, underlying how you can easily reach the countryside or the outskirts from Paris, as well as other amazing French cities, if you feel you need a break, a day off from the metropolis. "I like Paris being an international city, like my circle of friends. I love that, like in New York, where you can meet people from all over the world.

Placed on the Eastern side of the Palais de Tokyo, the **Museum of Modern Art of Paris** hosts important art collections of the 20th and 21st centuries.

The **Palais de Tokyo** welcomes great contemporary photographers exhibitions.

I also love Paris being the center of Europe: you can fly to other European cities in a few hours or leave the city in one hour. It can provide many opportunities to leave as well as to stay...."

Talking about Paris districts he says: "I don't have a favorite district. Maybe the 18th arrondissement. I find all the place de Clichy area interesting. But I can't figure out a favorite place. Paris is all fabulous. Paris appearance is awesome everywhere!", he says enthusiastically remembering where he usually walks. "If I think about a Parisian park, the Bois de Boulogne comes immediately to my mind. French people go walking there, but if they have a dog, they tend to walk it on the street or in the neighborhood, unless they live nearby the park. I noticed that... But I find it amazing to get lost in a park, watching passers-by or spotting unexpected and stolen moments", he ponders He's also passionate about something else in Paris. "Paris has excellent food and that's definitively another pleasure of the city. French food is well known and Parisian top restaurants standard is very high, maybe one of the highest in the world. Lower standard restaurants share the other European cities style, but the Parisian top quality food is actually excellent", he says, proving to be an extraordinary gourmet.

Erwitt believes that Paris is above all the capital of art he has been inspired by so much in his entire production. "I've always been fascinated by

art, I like contemporary art in general. I remember the Palais de Tokyo was a good destination. Frankly, I feel close to the 19th and 20th centuries painters like Soutine, Modigliani or Giacometti. I may be old fashioned, but I think that Robert Doisneau is a fantastic photographer. These are all iconic characters, they came before me, but they are artists I link with Paris, as icons. They will never fade and keep being fascinating", he says, without forgetting his passion about cinema. "My Paris is within the classic films of the 40s and beyond, like for example 'The Baker's Wife' and 'Knock', and with legendary actors like Louis Jouvet and Jacques Tati", he reminds, and carries on: "Among the most enchanting things in Paris there are many small cinemas in several districts that keep performing classic films. And that's really unique."

He thinks just one city may look like Paris, in some way: "I'm sure the only city comparing to Paris is Rome. Yes, Rome and Paris. They are definitively very different, but they both provide their visitors with their best, in artistic, food and lifestyle terms..." he reflects, going back to his life memories. As for the French capital he has always liked hanging out in, he's sure about one thing: "Paris is a city with good and bad times, easier and more difficult times, but there's a reason why it is called 'the city of the lights': even if they don't shine at hard times, they will surely shine back again."

**Cinematography**
From the top of the Arc de Triomphe you can admire the Parisian panorama that has often been immortalized in successful films.

# MICHEL GONDRY
## The Innovator

Paris is a wonderful place for him, between fantasy and reality. A microcosm made of real universes, as well as visionary one, created by his own imagination and creativity, with a dreamlike aesthetic displaying charmly in his music video clips and in his movies. They are romantic, unpredictable, involving, they lead you to another dimension out of mind and space boundaries. The director, screenwriter, producer and actor Michel Gondry is able to surprise throughout his art as much as Paris itself.

He picks things up from childhood, dreams and desires, using a splendid scenic design, digital effects and surreal as well as original visual expedients. Michel Gondry explores new horizons and his suggestions can be found among the hues of clouds floating in the wind, between sunrise and sunset. You can see the shades from a bridge of the Seine in a rainy day, in the steps on concrete, that seem to chase you in the blowing air among building walls. "Paris is wetter than the majority of the other cities. I see it gray and green", Gondry says and thinks between the memory of a city he loves and the worry for the video he has to shoot with Beyoncé the day after. "Actually I'm a bit nervous...", he underlines. All his production seems to pursue a moment, a thought difficult to grasp that stays in his mind because so beautiful.

He admits Paris has always been a source of inspiration and artistic experimentation, though now he lets him be inspired by overseas places like Los Angeles. But in Paris his first love for art sprung in all its forms. And his roots are here.

He was born in Versailles, on 8th May 1963. He has got passionate about pop music since he was a teenager and he moved to Paris, where he started his career as a drummer in the rock band Oui Oui. He was in charge of its video clips until 1992, when the band split up. Music and images will be part of his film production for ever and will mark it thanks to his special and magic originality.

His talent burst right from the start and one of his video broadcast on MTV was noticed by Bjork, an artist he would cooperate with for a long time. She asked him to direct "Human Behaviour". Meanwhile he started working with other great artists such as the Chemical Brothers and The White Stripes. He also shot important commercials. After having shot several short films, he became well-known with "Eternal Sunshine of the Spotless Mind" (2004) with Jim Carrey and Kate Winslet, winning the Golden Globe

> My favorite places in Paris are the same where I shot my films: the Gare de Lyon, the Palais des Mirages at the Musée Grévin and the Eiffel Tower.

The **Notre-Dame chimeras** watch the square below, as if it was one of Victor Hugo's imagined scene.

for the best original screenplay. In "The Science of Sleep" (2006), with Gael García Bernal and Charlotte Gainsbourg, he tells the story of a young man who has always had problems of distinguishing dreams from reality. After moving to Mexico with his father, he gets back to Paris when his father dies. Here he will encounter love, even if his suggestion for his imaginary world will grow.

Paris explodes in his artistic imagination especially with "Mood Indigo" (2013) starring Audrey Tautou and Romain Duris. The film talks about the surreal and poetic story of a man, Colin, an idealist who dreams of perfect love. He falls in love with the exquisite Chloé, a sweet girl acting as if she was the personification of a Duke Ellington's song. She loves him back and soon they get married, but the drama starts on their honeymoon. A flower blooms in her lungs and he beggars himself trying to save her. The only way to make her feel better is to surround her with fresh flowers, and other expensive and precious cares, everyday. He works until he breaks, until all the world around them crumbles.

Though the events are imaginary, Gondry makes use of narration to explore Paris as a director, with his own eyes. And especially the glimpses

Alain Ducasse's restaurant **Jules Verne**, on the Eiffel Tower second floor, represents a different way to enjoy the Parisian renowned monument.

"Climbing the Eiffel Tower to have lunch in the 'swing' restaurant is like finding yourself inside a magic kaleidoscope."

he's fond of. "My favorite places in Paris are the same where I shot this film: the Gare de Lyon, the Palais des Mirages at the Musée Grévin and the Eiffel Tower. They all remind me of strong and intense memories", he tells. The film is an adaptation of a Boris Vian's surreal story. A writer, a musician, and eccentric artist, a leading figure of Paris after the second post war; a friend of Camus and Sartre who introduced him to jazz with Duke Ellington and Miles Davis.

Gondry admits he has taken advantage of deeply exploring extremely evocative places, like the huge fresco featuring several cities inside the Gare de Lyon. And also, the Palais des Mirages at the Musée Grévin: a hall where Gondry admits he always discover something new and amazing and where he feels like being in another dimension, just like his own works. Climbing the Eiffel Tower to have lunch in the 'swing' restaurant he sometimes goes with friends or colleagues, is like finding yourself inside a magic kaleidoscope...

The view changes at any moment, extraordinarily. So the Eiffel Tower, though being a tourist and crowded destination, remains one of his favorite monuments in Paris. It shields a magic touch the director can always grasp in a new, different and special way.

Facing Gondry is like being carried inside one of his dreams and his universe.

What do you like best of Paris? And what do you dislike the most? "It's too slow, and it's too slow", he dares say, playing with the contradiction of what one may or may not like... he probably refers to the French capital relaxed rhythm compared to other big metropolises.

In Paris he likes hesitating. He suggests some destinations he usually goes to when in Paris. They have kept their authentic and characteristic spirit, in spite of time passing and modernity. "I don't go to hotels in Paris...", he acknowledges,

**The Train bleu**
This smart restaurant, inside the Gare de Lyon, was opened in 1901. Some films have been shot inside its halls.

The wax statues at the **Musée Grévin** which hosts the Palais des Mirages as well.

"The Palais des Mirages at the Musée Grévin: a hall where
I always discover something new and amazing and where
I feel like being in another dimension."

A renowned boulangerie in Montmartre or the **brasserie Le Cépage** in rue Caulaincourt
(on the right): there are plenty of opportunities for a leap into the Belle époque in Paris.

"Le Cépage, in Montmartre, is a brasserie, with a very lively bar
attended by artists, actors, directors and creative people."

unlike other film directors who attend hotel bars, have dinner or sleep in hotels. "As for restaurants I like the Au Virage, in rue Lepic, and Le Cépage bar, in rue Caulaincour", he confesses. The first is in Montmartre. It's an evocative atmosphere bistro with typical French gastronomy. The second is there as well. It's a brasserie, with a very lively bar attended by artists, actors, directors and creative people mingling with some tourists.

Each time, Michel Gondry tries to rediscover Paris from a different point of view, but he doesn't always succeed. "Sometimes I ride my bike to go around, but I've become lazy recently... I don't like sports", he says, though he admits he ventures himself on foot among the less known roads and corners. "If I go for a walk in Paris I go to the Parc des Buttes-Chaumont", he adds. This wonderful public garden, placed in the North-East of the city, is the third biggest park of Paris and was built in 1867 under Napoleon III's commission. It keeps a great variety of exotic plants, some of them grow on the romantic

lake banks, and it's full of birds. It's like being in another world, you climb Sibilla's small temple shaping a mystic pentagon and you can enjoy a beautiful view of the French capital. You really feel far from anything. That's maybe why Gondry is enthusiastic about it. Maybe that's the dimension he misses most, when he spends time in Los Angeles on business under the Californian sun. He feels melancholic about his city for several reasons, but when he's far away, he especially misses one thing: "The main difference between Los Angeles and Paris is that in America you always need a car... but in Paris you can walk everywhere!", Gondry states.

Paris provides excellent opportunities for **bike** rides along the Seine, for example, to enjoy some exclusive sights of its main monuments.

Velib' **bike sharing** service started in 2007 and has registered an increasing number of users. One of its hire points is in front of the Hotel de Ville.

"Sometimes I ride my bike to go around,
but I've become lazy recently...
I don't like sport."

# ISABELLE HUPPERT

## The Art of Acting Lover

Acting is part of her very soul, which she is able to transfigure like she does with her face and body, turning into many different women with a perfect realism that makes you forget this is fiction. When you make a film, she once stated, it's not just a matter of artistic expression, but of expressing yourself. She usually favors unusual, conspicuous as well as difficult and unpredictable roles: she doesn't fear challenges, she's brave in all her choices like a great actress is. She believes that acting in films and in plays, where all is more immediate, is a great adventure. With the same passion she has been able to involve her audience in wonderful journeys in search of different humanity's facets.

Isabelle Huppert faces her Paris with the same intensity. She was born here on 16th March 1953, she is fond of Paris and deeply attached to it. As a soul guide, she leads you to discover deep down to the less known or taken for granted twists and turns, revealing an unexpected and personal view, as awesome as her art. "I love Paris, I think I am lucky to have lived here for a long time and I often say it's a pretty extraordinary city to look at and to live in. It's the city where you can work at things best, amuse yourself, like going to the

> It is a city that has incredible potential, you never get bored in Paris!

theater, to the cinema, or to museums. It has incredible potential, you never get bored in Paris!", she says enthusiastically.

Isabelle spent her childhood in Ville-d'Avray and approached acting when she was really young, supported by her mother, an English teacher, and by those who were close to her as well as won by her natural talent.

"I was raised in the Western *banlieu* in Paris and my first memories recall when I used to go and see my grandmothers living in Paris. Therefore my childhood memories go back to the 16th arrondissement, like the Bois de Boulogne, and the 9th arrondissement", she refers to her first impression of the city. As for her education, she attended the Versailles Conservatoire, where she was awarded an acting prize, and the Conservatoire National Supérieur d'Art Dramatique (CNSAD), in Paris.

She soon started a career in drama, which is still her passion, whereas she officially entered cinema in 1972 with "Faustine et le Bel Été", debuting in America with "Heaven's Gate" (1980), by Michael Cimino. Since then, her career has been rising. Above all, Isabelle is choosy about her screenplays and directors, she loves

"Maybe one of the building I like best is the Louvre: its square, magnificent and well proportioned courtyard, just like Bach's music."

great cinema, in its highest acting roles. She worked with lots of directors, such as Bertrand Tavernier, Jean-Luc Godard, Otto Preminger, Joseph Losey, Claude Chabrol, Marco Ferreri, Michael Haneke. But also: Paolo and Vittorio Taviani, Benoît Jacquot, Olivier Assayas, François Ozon, the renowned American director David O. Russel, Patrice Chéreau, Claire Denis, Anne Fontaine, Marco Bellocchio... not to mention many others like Christophe Honoré. Isabelle likes experimenting as many other artists marking history and collective memory do. Among her recent production: "Louder Than Bombs" (2015) by Joachim Trier, "Macadam Stories" (2016) by Samuel Benchetrit, "Things to Come" (2016) by Mia Hansen-Løve and "Elle" (2016) by Paul Verhoeven. She keeps being a very prolific drama artist; a passion she shares with many other Parisians, as

The **Louvre** is visited by more than 8 million people every year: many of them pass through Hall Napoléon, a big hall under the glass pyramid.

Many restaurants in **Saint-Germain-des-Près** have kept the Art Nouveau style of the early 20th century.

# Paris is a pretty extraordinary city to look at and to live in.

she admits. She was awarded the Molière Prize five times, thanks to her intense interpretation, such as in "Medea", directed by Jacques Lassalle, or in Ibsen's "Hedda Gabler" at the Odéon-Théâtre de l'Europe in Paris. She stood out abroad, as well, debuting in London with "Maria Stuarda" in 1996 and in New York, in 2006, with "4.48 Psychosis", gaining great success in 2014 with "The Maids", together with Cate Blanchett.

Isabelle has been married with the writer, producer and director Ronald Chammah since 1982 and they have three children. Their daughter Lolita Chamman is an actress and played together with her mother in "Copacabana" in 2010.

Isabelle is fascinated by Paris in its many opportunities to watch plays or movies. "Parisian theaters are split in two categories: funded and private ones. They both offer a wide selection of programs. The funded cinemas are more ambitious, while the private ones are more entertaining. I love juggling between the two. Paris is the best city for cinema lovers. You can watch recent or art-house films and there are often festivals or film shooting. I took charge of a cinema in Paris myself: the former 'Action Christine' in rue Christine, called 'Christine 21', currently run by my son. I like going there for old movies re-editions, for example John Ford's films, which I had the chance to rediscover", she says. Then she pauses and adds: "In Paris, you

From "Le Bon Marché" department store (on the left), to the fabric temple of the "**Marché Saint-Pierre**" (on the right), Paris can meet all tastes.

can watch the most different movies, anytime, both in small and big halls."

In addition to a wide and various production, Isabelle is one of the few actresses who has won the major prizes in global festivals: best actress in Cannes with "Violette Nozière" and "The Piano Teacher", in 1978 and 2001, the Volpi Cup for the best female interpretation at Venice Film Festival with "Story of Women" and "La Cérémonie", in 1988 and 1995, and a Silver Bear at Berlin Festival with "8 Women". In Paris, in 2005, she was awarded a special Golden Lion for "Gabrielle". Among her many recognitions, she won the BAFTA prize in 1978 as best actress with "The Lacemaker", she was nominated for the César Prize several times,

once winning with "La Cérémonie" (1995), she got two European Film Awards, one as best actress and another as best career, two Donatello's David, a Silver Ribbon and many other global awards. She was also appointed Knight of the Legion of Honor in 1999 and promoted as Officer in 2009. With her passionate and unblemished zeal, her acting art and boundless talent won't stop here.

When she thinks back of the way cinema has performed the French capital, she picks out the works portraying this metropolis best: a city that has always enthralled cinema greatest artists and masters: "There are loads of films showing Paris, even though they were shot in studios for

The **Galeries Lafayette**, the department store on boulevard Haussmann, is a tourist attraction and purchase destination.

a while. The Nouvelle Vague films showed the real Paris for the first time. 'Breathless' (1960) by Godard, and Chabrol's movies display a new way of shooting the city and the reality of the time. Jean Seberg walking along the Champs-Élysées in 'Breathless' is unforgettable."

She has special thoughts in terms of her source of inspiration: "I can't say Paris inspires me as an actress, I believe it's mainly a directors' source of inspiration. They shoot it in different ways whether they are French or foreigners. A foreign director watches and inspects the city from a different point of view, according to his or her sensitivity. Anyway it's nice to see a city you know well, shot by a great director, since the perspective is always so personal. Each time you rediscover Paris in a different way, throughout an artist's subjective look."

The **great glass** dome on top of their central hall was designed in Art Nouveau style by Ferdinand Chanut in 1912.

The **Philharmonic** at the Parc de la Villette, planned by Jean Nouvel, was inaugurated in 2015.

Isabelle owns an intimate view of Paris, far away from a tourist one: "You are often lazy in your city. When you visit a foreign city, you rush to the well known monuments, as when you get to New York and you go straight to the Empire State Building. I've never gone up to the third floor of the Eiffel Tower and I might have gone to the Arc de Triomphe once, but I'm not sure! It's not that easy to have a tourist soul in your own city! Maybe one of the building I like best is the Louvre: its square, magnificent and well proportioned court-yard, just like Bach's music, is pure classicism. And then, when you enter the museum, you discover such an extraordinary surrounding. There is an amazing full view of the Seine, you are over-whelmed by beauty", she admits in her personal and direct manner.

Talking about the city districts, she says: "I don't have a favorite district. I've lived on the left side of the Seine for a long time. Everyone tends to stay in their own districts. Paris is culturally very rich and I love hanging around other districts. I like changing, going to different places where I don't usually go. Some districts have changed a lot recently. For example, just think about the development around the Bibliotheque Nationale, in the 13th arrondisse-ment", she says. As for the city changes, she states: "Paris has changed, definitively. Some districts have developed: there are many migrations to the city center as well as movements to the outskirts.

Life moves to somewhere else, the city decentralizes and new districts grow", she underlines. She believes that Paris evolution has turned the city into something different from other European and global environments thanks to its own peculiarity: "A city like Paris changes and evolves continuously. Not as strikingly as New York or other American cities, where new buildings and new districts rise in three month time. Paris changes are slow, but they are deep and revolutionize the city. Paris is alive, it renews itself and regrows. Points of interest move. In north Paris there are la Villette and the Philarmonie."

Then Isabelle quotes some places she finds particularly fascinating and appealing: "I love Saint Pierre market, though I don't go there very often. You can buy some excellent fabrics. There are great stores in Paris, like the currently luxury Bon Marché, the Galeries Lafayette or le Printemps. I have a thing for the Saint Pierre market, in the 18th arrondissement, under the Butte Montmartre, as I said.

The surrounding area is pleasant, there are many restaurants, while the market provides a *savoir-faire* and handicraft atmosphere with all its fabrics and materials. You can only go there on foot, I hope it won't lose its authentic and old fashioned flair."

The **Philharmonic** concert hall is hosted in a building covered in aluminium and made of inclined planes.

The **Great Arche de La Défense**, is covered in Carrara white marble.

Thinking about Paris in the future, she expresses her wishes "I'd like the city to keep being alive and creative. Right now, Paris is slightly less active at night, but I'm optimistic", she says in her sparkling and positive manner that makes her even more attractive. You can perceive her energy flowing. In the same charming and articulated way, she tells about her ideas of Paris, as she sees it every day: "A color for Paris? A rainbow!", she states, revealing her deep love for her city. Just like her, you can't tell Paris in only one way. It's a bewitching parade of emotions, feelings, hues, shades, facets, transforming and enchanting, like a magic, amazing kaleidoscope.

**The Villette**
The Cité des sciences et de l'industrie is the biggest European museum complex in terms of science and technology.

# JEAN-PIERRE JEUNET

## The Great Enchanter

He's a great narrator, he enchants you while you listen; like a snake charmer's spell. His words are flowing and you just have to follow them, as he drags spectators into his films, like inside a kaleidoscope made of tiny colorful particles: perspective and images change any moment by watching inside. The whole becomes even more interesting when his adrift characters are revealed, in search of love or of a meaning for life. They are warm, full of emotion, at times crazed or ingenuous, still deeply human and convincing. The film director, screen writer and producer Jean-Pierre Jeunet shoots films, set in Paris where you can discover his picture of the city. He considers it a unique place in the world: surrealist, romantic, comic and amusing, highly contemplative. "When you live abroad and step back in Paris, you stay wordless or utter: 'Jeez! It's one of the most beautiful cities in the world', together with Venice, Amsterdam, San Francisco and Rome… But Paris is divine like its train stations. I love them. I still remember when, once back in Paris after twenty months in Los Angeles, I had the same feeling of wonder I had when I got here for the first time", he admits in a passionate voice.

> I adore the Eiffel Tower, such a huge block of metal, and its punk side, timeless.

Jeunet gets excited when he thinks about the first time he saw Paris: "My first memory of Paris…. It was summer, I was 19 or 20 years old, I was doing my military service. With a friend we decided to set off for a week in Paris. I remember wandering along the streets. I was really excited since I knew I would get back here after the Army, to try my luck within the cinema industry. It was all new, a kind of magic. I had visited Paris, but I was a kid. That time was different instead. In my first months in Paris, I would feel astonished and blessed each time I discovered a secret corner of the city or just when I would get off the metro. I used to feel stoned and euphoric along the streets, like in rue Mouffetard in the Latin District, for example. And I felt free after my military service. So I remember those months as the most beautiful time of my life", he lets his memory go and his words are full of irrepressible enthusiasm.

Jeunet comes from the Loire, Roanne, where he was born on 3rd September 1953. He admits he has always had cinema and films in his blood: when he was seventeen he started working at the French postal service and made money to buy his first 8mm camera.

The **Café des Deux Moulins** in Pigalle, where Amélie, the protagonist of the well known Jeunet's film, works as a waitress.

Experimenting short films, he learned and deepened animation techniques at the Cinémation Studios. He met the director, screen writer, cartoonist and designer Marc Caro. It was a lucky chance for Jeunet. They started a profitable cooperation leading him to carry out his first short films like "L'Évasion" and "Le Manège". He was awarded the César Prize in 1981. After having directed many commercials and music videos, he gained two César recognitions for the short films "Pas de Repos pour Billy Brakko", inspired by Caro's comics, and "Foutaises". Here he started an important partnership with an actor who would play in many of his films: Dominique Pinon. His international reputation came with films like "Delicatessen" (1991) and "The City of Lost Children" (1995), so that the 20th Century Fox commissioned

his first film of the science fiction saga Alien, "Alien Resurrection" (1991). He broke the record, with "Amélie" (2001) where Jeunet portrayed the city he loves best and has chosen to live in, winning the European Film Awards as the best director. The film tells Amélie's life. The protagonist works as a waitress in a Paris café in Montmartre and enjoys helping others in their search for love and happiness, with a taste for life pleasures. Then, Jeunet worked at other projects increasing his artist and visionary fame: "A Very Long Engagement" (2004) is based on Sébastien Japrisot's story, "Micmacs" (2009), with Dany Boon and "The Young and Prodigious Spivet" (2013). A special ability in catching details and observing people is revealed in these films. A feature Jeneut rediscovers again and again in his Paris.

"I don't love monuments on their own. It's not a matter of monuments or landscape... I'm not so sensitive with monuments...I'm more keen on papers kiosks, indoor and outdoor metro stations, I look for details, like in Jacques Tardi's comics. I'm fond of a wholeness of tiny things rather than monuments. For instance, Montmartre is a district I know well, but I've never wanted to visit the Basilica of the Sacre Coeur. It reminds me of Jean Renoir in his journey to India, together with François Truffaut, to shoot 'The River'. They didn't want to visit the Taj Mahal, they weren't interested in it. I've the same way to see things. I'm not interested in monuments when I explore a city. Obviously, I adore the Effeil Tower, such a huge block of metal, and its punk side, timeless. It's lost in the middle of the city, like a platform floating on the high seas. That's what I called 'the Eiffel effect'. I also love the Canal Saint-Martin with the Port de l'Arsenal and its wonderful boats. When I walk along it, I always think about 'Hôtel du Nord' by Marcel Carné, a director I admire and who inspired my film 'Micmacs'" he says, sinking in a flow of thoughts that, he admits, run along his creative mind when he thinks of Paris.

"Has Paris inspired my films? It depends... For example 'A Very Long Engagement' is an adaptation of Sebastien Japrisot's book. 'Micmacs' is rather a cartoon for kids. On the other hand, 'Amélie' is the result of twenty-

**Amélie**
Nearby the Café des Deux Moulins, there is Monsier Collignon's bakery as well, another shop made famous by Jeunet's film.

> "I also love the Canal Saint-Martin with the Port de l'Arsenal and its wonderful boats."

five years of memories and written notes. The film gathers small anecdotes and oddities, details picked up by my work partner Guillame Laurant. We are a nice duet, since we both have a peculiar idea of details and an exclusive way to find good anecdotes. Our next project will cover sensuality and sex, but we want to provide the film with an anticonformist atmosphere, a humorous and funny note, like in 'Amélie'. Just like the dwarf in the garden Amélie like taking pictures with, acting as if he traveled around the world: he has left traces and has become an urban legend. I tend to imagine another urban legend like this, but with a different plot", Jeunet reveals, carrying on.

"If I think of a film that describes my city, I recall 'Last Tango in Paris' by Bernardo Bertolucci, but also 'The Conformist' where you can see the Musée d'Orsay like a station, as it was at that time. To honor such a director, I shot a scene of 'Micmacs' using the same framing. I also love Marcel Carné or Jacques Prevert's Paris of 'Bizarre, Bizarre' and 'Port of Shadows'. I'm a fan of them and I have the whole collection of their objects in my office. Other special places of Paris are those of 'Amélie', like Canal Saint-Martin, its small bridges and the exquisite bateaux, the mythical Hotel du Nord and the nearby train station", he goes on, revealing details of his education like the films he saw, films that helped him develop his artistic vision and love the

French capital even more. "My film 'Amélie' is set in Montmartre, I adore this district. It's a small village inside the city. It's out of time, completely detached by the rest. That's why all Amélie's story develops there. But I incorporated what I love best of Paris in all my three films set in Paris: the places and the details I'm enthralled by in a special way. Therefore, If you want to find out what I like in Paris, just watch my films! For instance I've always loved the Galeries Lafayette crystal roof, as you can see in 'Micmacs'." He carries on and describes what he likes best of the district he works and lives in, his biggest source of inspiration, despite the fact that he's extremely familiar with it.

"Generally speaking I appreciate Montmartre as I live here. It's a sort of small universe inside the metropolis, rich in mysterious characters who own their own life and history. I've placed some of them in 'Amélie', as the red dressed widow or the other unusual characters. I never get tired of this district. Sometimes I do, with Paris, but never with Montmartre. On Sundays, I walk my dog here and I always get excited. Moreover, the buildings don't resemble each other and I have the feeling of being in a German expressionist film. I've always lived in Montmartre, two hundred meters far from the café where Amélie works, the Café des Deux Moulins.

The ships that cross the Seine and the Canal Saint-Martin dock at **Port de l'Arsenal**, once a wharf. The basin surrounding the Bastille fortress used to be here.

My office is here, too. I would like to organize an exhibition of the numerous objects I own and have collected over the years, one day. I have a multitude of objects, they're extraordinary! And I would like to plan it right here", he admits.

"Another place I adore in Montmartre is Studio 28, an old district cinema, worked out by Jean Cocteau. Here I shot a sequence of 'Amélie'. It's a one minute walk from home. It's easy to go there. It's a quiet and pretty isolated place and has a good selection of films. Definitively not commercial ones. It has also high standard technical conditions. I'm a real fan of this place!" he carries on, revealing some personal taste beyond his characters' ones. "There's a flea market at the Bastille… I prefer going there to come upon small old-time images or paintings. Any time I go there I buy something. It's one of my best places and times in Paris", he reveals. Without being a big fan of museums, he admits there's one he finds charming, after all: "If I had to pick out a museum, I would choose the Musée d'Orsay. It's an old station and one of my favorite places. I also like Haussmann's architecture providing the city with a lot of style. Paris has a peculiar and strong personality", he says, carrying on with his explanations: "I favor the Musée d'Orsay as I'm a great fan of classic painting, Expressionism and figurative art. Besides, I can't stand contemporary art, despite its being fashionable nowadays. And people get crazy about it, but I find it

**The Gare de Lyon**
The 67 meter high tower of the train station displays the biggest clock in Paris that still keeps its original mechanisms.

The **Gare du Nord** is one of the main train stations of Paris and transit point for millions of travelers every year.

too commercial. I have the feeling of being in a sect, with sorts of guru coming to sell their works. I love getting lost inside impressionist paintings at the Musée d'Orsay, instead", he states frankly, as typical as his personality.

Just like his Amélie, discovering pleasures in Paris, again and again. Among them, gastronomy: "I love French brasseries. They aren't fashionable, as they often catch tourists. The Parisians prefer the so-called bistrot gourmand, a new concept of brasserie, more expensive and with a less traditional cuisine. But I belong to the brasserie habitués and I like having breakfast there. In particular at Le Grand Colbert, definitively one of my favorite place. Paris is enchanting, especially at Christmas. I always eat seafood at the brasseries. But there are also numer-

ous restaurants in the heart of Montmartre. Every day at noon I have lunch at La Midinette, a few steps far from my home and office. Food is home made. It's small and evocative in here", suggesting how to live like locals in Paris. "The cuisine is very French, typical, traditional, in the brasseries. Not light for sure, but definitively delicious. I prefer not having dinner, but 'filling my bellies' in a brasserie at lunchtime", he adds straightaway, satisfied.

Jeunet owns his way to venture in Paris. "I have a scooter, an old BMW model, a vintage motorbike you don't see around anymore. When I was younger I used to cycle. Unfortunately, one day I found my bike with a completely broken wheel.... At that time I was poor and fixing it was too expensive. I remember I started crying in the street, while passers-by

Paris is made magic not only by its artificial lights, but also by the sun rays reflecting on the buildings, the Seine water and the monuments.

were walking in front of what remained of my bike. Therefore I prefer a scooter, more practical and enduring", he says, stating he still takes pleasure from the wind blowing on his face and from images as well as city glimpses running in front of his eyes.

"My only advice to an artist in Paris is to do it for the sake of doing, without thinking about the result. Who cares. Firstly you need to feel proud and happy about your creation. That really matters the most. It's the philosophy of life I adopted by debuting in cinema. Even today, after all these years, I keep creating for the sake of doing it and that's the same with my personal life. I love things becoming alive. I happen to shape animals from natural objects and such an artistic activity kind of satisfies me. Nowadays, art has become accessible to everybody. Any-

one can make a film with the help of a mobile or a pc. But you always need to ask yourself: do I want to be a director or an inventor? In other words, would I rather be or do? That's the fundamental question when you want to start a career within cinema", he explains, thinking of all the other artists who chose to live in Paris, like him.

"A color for Paris? It depends. As a director I feel like a painter playing with colors. With 'Amélie' we used warm colors: yellow, green, red. I love using different hues just like an artist's palette. That's what Bernardo Bertolucci did in his film. 'Last Tango in Paris'. Its roads were shot in deep winter with blue and gray hues and a predominant color: a vivid twilight orange. It's divine. I don't like using such a term, but as an artist, I own a personal view of

Paris and that's my Paris. Whereas another artist -may see it in another way. The colors of my Paris are 'Amélie''s ones", he admits, thinking about the shades representing his city best; he might use them if he had to paint, one day.

If he thinks of a smell recalling the French capital, he says, instead: "When I walk along the several districts, - I come across thousands of smells and flavors, from the restaurants, kitchens, boulangeries, boutiques and passers-by... But you should ask my dog Specer, an Australian shepherd, he's got an excellent sniff. He's old, but I take him out in nature, to the Bois de Boulogne or the Bois de Vincennes. He's a lucky dog. These parks have endless and splendid woods", he says. Here, in the glimpses of nature stolen from the metropolis, Jeunet can "breathe" Paris together with his adorable and friendly dog.

He gives a glance to the future of his city, thinking of the possibility that one day he might get the inspiration for a new film entirely set in Paris: "I would like to see more skyscrapers in Paris like in London, where tradition and innovation melt together. Changes in Paris are slow, that's a shame. In France, we are still very conservative", he admits in a funny yet bitter way. "In the future I believe the Parisians will move to the outskirts and the banlieues, the surrounding suburbs. I'm

Placed near the Palais-Royal, **Le Grand Colbert** restaurant owns its name to Louis XIV's ministry and is renowned for its elegant furniture as well as for its food.

afraid this city may lose its dynamism, its energy. I wouldn't want to see Paris turning into a museum, crowded by tourists", he says worried, but still hopefully.

Basically he owns a visionary and romantic dream exciting the hearts of the noblest and most sensitive characters. An evocative dream for humanity and history, like a real artist owns. "When I dream of Paris, I imagine it in mid August, when the Parisians leave the city and chaos leaves room to peace and tranquility. It's the only time you can go around easily, riding a scooter in the summer sun. I would like to see my city always like that. But I must admit that my favorite month is March, when the metropolis is in bloom and Spring starts! Or I like Autumn, when leaves fall! March is giboulées time, sudden rainfalls leaving room to an exquisite sky full of beautiful clouds. I find it amazing! I'm lucky also because I've a house with a big garden and in March it's really fabulous! Lilacs grow in here too, my favorite flowers, with an incredible smell, providing the surrounding landscape with a touch of violet magic!", he admits, revealing his Parisian personal universe. "As far as I'm concerned, I wish my city could offer me some new places, sooner or later. I've loved it so much, keep researching but everything has become complicated! But, I wouldn't give up, after all. I know there will always be new corners and details to discover in this city", he states balancing thoughts and still hoping for a new great dream: crumbling again in the magic spell of Paris.

157

# CHARLOTTE LE BON

## The Creative Artist

She's gifted with grace and talent which reveal intensively on the screen. It's a pleasure to talk to her, since her mind is a continuous flow of ideas, artistic suggestions and creative thoughts. Charlotte Le Bon is an artist, drawer, illustrator, and one of the best emerging, most intense and deepest actresses of the new generation, who has been able to stand out in Hollywood and in France. Despite being Canadian, she decided to settle in Paris which she finds one of the most magic places in the world. You can spot her love for the city in her arts, photographs, street art and drawings, like in the project where she is portrayed with huge hearts in several localities, especially in her Paris.

In the image "JUST NEEDS A REST - HEART-HEADED PROJECT" she is sleeping by a wall in Montmartre. A girl with a heart shaped head is drawn on it. Another shot, in Paris, illustrates a crown of pink flowers on a wall depicting the peace symbol, while she holds a sign "REMEMBER CHARLIE". She took this picture a week after the public demonstration gathering more than three million people in Paris streets, after the terrorist attack at the weekly satirical magazine *Charlie Hebdo*. Such an event deeply marked Parisian history. In other areas of Paris, you can spot her in eccentric moments when she is playing with the "Décrochez la Lune" collages: a huge moon is tied with a rope all around her acting as if she was pulling it towards her. Similar motives, as well as other creative and unique ones, are found in her works, like in her serigraphs.

> I like to think it wasn't me who chose this city, but Paris who chose me.

"I'm Canadian, I was born and grew up in Montreal, but I've lived in Paris for more than six years. I like to think it wasn't me who chose this city, but Paris who chose me. I got here to work as a model and then I found a job in a daily show where I used to write and play in sketches. I worked out 200 sketches, broadcast for a year at dinner time. At that time, becoming an actress wasn't even a choice for me, it just happened. Now, that's my life and I love it."

She's actors Brigitte Paquette and Richard Le Bon's daughter. Born in Montreal on 4th September 1986, she started working as a model since she was sixteen. She left Canada when she was nineteen, carrying on with the profession in France and all over the world. As she admits now, however, her soul and attitudes weren't really close to the world of fashion at

the time. Acting was burning in her artist's heart. So, in 2010, she started her TV career as "Miss Météo" on French Canal +, in *Le Grand Journal* talk show, and then as a reporter in the *Petit Journal*. Meanwhile, she kept her interested in cinema and drawing. After having played in some short films, she played roles in films like "Asterix and Obelix: God Save Britannia", "Mood Indigo", by Michel Gondry, "Yves Saint Laurent" – a biopic on the well known fashion designer where she plays the role of the muse Victoire Doutreleau – and "The Hundred-Foot Journey" by Lasse Hallström.

She was noticed in Europe and in America, she keeps splitting herself between Europe and overseas, still extremely close to her Paris she considers home just like Montreal. In 2015 she played in "The Walk" by Robert Zemeckis, interpreting Annie Allix, Philippe Petit's girlfriend (Joseph Gordon-Levitt); he is the well known French tightrope walker who, on 7th August 1974, crossed the distance between the World Trade Center Twin Towers with no protection, on a steel cable. In 2016, she played

**Barbès**

The Barbès well-known and popular district, around the same name boulevard of the 18th arrondissement, is served by the 4 metro line.

"The Marché des Enfants Rouges,
the oldest covered market in town,
where you can eat all you want."

The **Marché des Enfants Rouge**, in Marais district, is Paris oldest covered market.

**Graffiti and murales**, chosen to decorate some trendy bars, represent a new artistic bloom is some city areas.

"I live in Barbès that is still known
as a little dangerous district. Apart from that,
it's colorful like a Parisian Harlem."

in "Bastille Day", an action film with Idris Elba, "Project Lazarus", a thriller and futuristic drama with Tom Hughes, "Anthropoid", the true story of two Czech soldiers sent to kill SS chief Reinhard Heydrich in 1942, "Le Secret des Banquises" with Guillaume Canet, and "The Promise" with Christian Bale and Oscaar Isaac, telling the love triangle among a medicine student, an American journalist living in Paris and a beautiful woman, during the last days of the Ottoman Empire.

Charlotte admits her life has turned into a beautiful dream and Paris is part of it.

"I live in Barbès, that is still known as a little dangerous district. Apart form that, it's colorful like a Parisian Harlem. I changed many apartments when I got in Paris. I don't feel like having found the one I consider home yet, but I'm sure you need to try many different things before", she says referring to her experience in the city and her willingness to experiment all in a creative and artistic way. She is natural born curious.

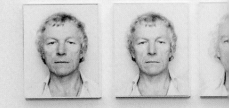

As for her favorite districts, she states: "Marais is probably the best place to walk and spot interesting galleries like Emmanuel Perrotin, Yvon Lambert or Anne-Dominique Toussaint's Galerie Cinema, where I held my first exhibition in September 2016. It's close to the Marché des Enfants Rouges, the oldest covered market in town, where you can eat all you want", she says thinking of what she likes best of the city. This market is a real institution, full of atmosphere and suggestions. It was so called in memory of an old near orphanage that used to have the children dressed in red. It's the most ancient market in Paris, build on Louis XIII's request for Marais district in 1615. It's open all days, except on Monday, and stretches from rue de Bretagne to all the Marais area; the Parisians

**The Galerie Yvon Lambert**
Placed in rue Vieille-du-Temple, Yvon Lambert's gallery of contemporary art displays American and European artists' works.

The **International Fair of Contemporary Art** (FIAC) has taken place every year in Paris since 1974.
It's a meeting point for art dealers, collectors and museums coming from all over the world.

> "Walking along the Seine at night makes you feel like when you're about to open a present."

love it and call it "place du village" because of its convivial flair. It sells fruit and vegetables, fresh and ethnic products. You can buy the food and eat it outdoors like in a multi-ethnic sidewalk café.

"I have many favorite monuments in Paris. The city itself is a monument! I've always been an Eiffel Tower fan, especially when it shines through its lights. It's awesome! I still can't understand why so many people might have hated it when it was built", Charlotte comments thinking back of Paris architectural beauty. But there's something of Paris leaving her breathless: "Walking along the Seine at night makes you feel like when you're about to open a present."

**Berges**
The pedestrian area along the left bank of the Seine stretches from the Musée d'Orsay to the Pont de l'Alma and is a new way to enjoy the city.

# CLAUDE LELOUCH

## A Fan of Love

He admits the more he knows Paris, the more he appreciates life. He's sure that if you love Paris, it will love you back, like a passionate lover. Sometimes he feels like a scientific laboratory observer studying existence, passion, emotions, lies, betrayals. An extraordinary experience. The great director, screen writer and producer Claude Lelouch represents a myth of cinema and proves to have such a magic sensitivity in relating with his city he displays through his work.

"Paris is of all colors! Thanks to its melting hues, its boundlessness, its marvelous buildings, its changeable weather... You can spot four seasons in the same day. In people's heart Paris is especially linked with red, the color of passion and love. Paris is often associated with love!", he states, evoking his cinema that was able to win people's heart and the whole world.

His relationship with the city is deeply personal. "Paris is a wonderful city, it's really special. It's a metropolis but also a human dimension and a full of fashion city. The districts look like connected villages bond together like in a beautiful puzzle. Each piece ends up in its right place", he thinks, underlying that's aroused his curiosity since he was a child.

> Paris is a wonderful city, it's really special.
> It's a metropolis but also a human dimension and a full of fashion city.

Son of a Jewish businessman and tailor whose family had lived in Algeria for at least three generations, Claude Lelouch was born in Paris on 30th October 1937. He got interested in cinematography since he was a kid and he used to spend his time at the cinema.

After having been influenced by a movie, he wondered whether he could meet the actors behind the scenes, as if they were really there. The scenes used to leave him with real impressions...

Stories like films entered his blood up to the point that when he graduated, he asked his father to buy him a camera to travel around the world and shoot documentaries. So his adventure in cinematography began.

When he was thirteen he released his first work and in 1954 he displayed his short film "Le Mal du Siècle" at Cannes Amateur Film Festival.

A professional director since 1956, his military service between 1957 and 1960 didn't deflect his attention from the path he chose to follow.

Meanwhile he shot more than two hundred "scopitones", short jukebox musicals, and TV commercials. He also founded his production company, Les Films.

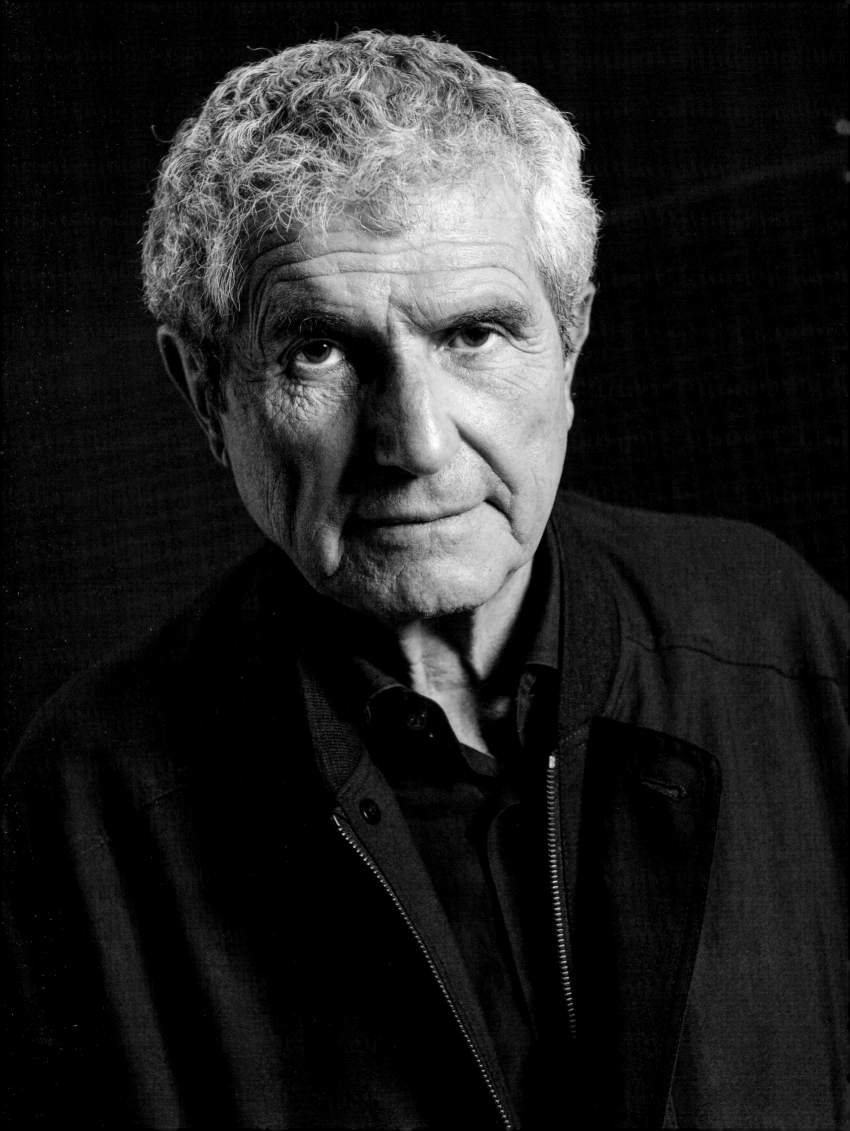

> "Paris is of all colors!
> Thanks to its melting
> hues and its
> boundlessness."

His first movie is dated 1960, "Le Propre de L'Homme" which he played in, wrote and produced. But he became internationally successful in 1966 with the direction of "A Man and A Woman" winning two Golden Globe and the Palme d'Or in Cannes. It's an extraordinary love story, of a man and a woman both losing their loved ones. They meet, their feelings grow and new emotions develop. His sensitivity is touching in his shootings, hesitating moments and details showing deep humanity.

Lelouch himself admits he learned from his city how to love so deeply. And intensively, at high speed... he says: "I was born and grew up in Paris. I've always felt myself as a Parisian. I told my city best in my ten minutes short film 'C'Était Un

**The Arc de Triomphe**
Initially meant to celebrate Napoleon's victories, the arch closing the Champs-Élysèes is currently a French universal landmark.

Rendez-Vous', released in 1976, in a sample of ciné-ma-vérité." He keeps explaining his experience: "It's a drive at full speed in Paris, passing by some of its most important monuments like the Arc de Triomphe, the Opéra Garnier, Place de la Concorde with its obelisk and the Champs-Élyséés, Pigalle. It's a challenge for pedestrians, red traffic lights, pigeons and everything standing in the path. In the last scene, the car is parked in Montmartre. On the background, the well known Basilica of the Sacre Coeur and the encounter with a woman. That's Paris: it leaves you breathless", he explains. The director then remembers that the city hasn't really changed in its essence, though passing time and a natural evolution. Its soul counts most and it makes everything unforgettable. "The picture of Paris in the 70s shot in my short film 'C'Était Un Rendez-Vous', is not that far away from contemporary Paris. Even though today is a harder time, what makes Paris is still there: its light heartedness, its beauty... they were there forty years ago. And I hope they will stay there in forty years time", he admits.

Lelouch is not ashamed of facing challenges in his artistic production. He had

**The Opéra Garnier**
The Palais Garnier, a Second Empire style building culminates with the sculptures of Apollo, Poetry and Music, by Aimé Millet (1860-1869).

172

There are **fountains**, dedicated to **rivers and seas**, in Place de la Concorde.

several problems with the authorities and was even arrested because of the eight minutes reckless driving of this short film, an hymn to Paris. But he loves experimenting and can go deeply, searching for humanity essence and its boundaries. In pursuit of an unrestrained passion, almost uncontrollable.

All his films followed this direction, towards an exploration of love, relationships, existences. They meet and cross. They don't know where to go or end. You can discover him in "Live for Life" (1967), "Toute Une Vie" (1974), "À Nous Deux" (1979), "Les Uns et les Autres" (1981), while he gained great success in 1996 with "Les Misérables" (from Victor Hugo's novel) winning the Golden Globe. Lelouch carried on his research and exploration of the relationship between sex and romanticism, like in recent works like "Les Parisiens" (2004), "Salaud, On T'Aime!" (2014) and "Un + Une (2015)".

The director confesses that his interest for such a dimension

**Place de la Concorde**
The obelisk standing in the middle of the square is one of the two, erected by Pharaoh Ramesses II at the entrance of the Luxor temple, and a present to France by Egypt in 1833.

"My favorite district remains Montmartre
due to its lively and young atmosphere,
and to the many artists distinguishing it."

didn't make him disregard Paris and his people. "The Parisians are a universe on their own, they can enjoy life, but in the end they lack a sense of humor", he explains, confiding in what makes Paris even more attractive in his eyes. "What make Paris very special are its beautiful girls. You can see them in the squares, along the road, in the wonderful parks and gardens... sitting and chatting on the benches. You can discover some of the most beautiful women in the world!" he ensures and shows the sensitivity he's always displayed in grasping the feminine soul within his films. As if he was able to understand the female soul in all its shades.

Then he thinks about his favorite places from a personal and artistic point of view. "My favorite district is still Montmartre, due to its lively and young atmosphere, and to the many artists distinguishing it. I like its bakeries, cafés and bars. And here there is one of my favorite restaurants, Le Coq Rico. It's a real original bistro, with delicious gastronomy", he says. He's enthusiastic about his district being inhabited by many artists fortune seekers with a dream to fulfill.

**Montmartre**
To climb Montmartre hill there is an inclined elevator, but if you choose to climb the stairs you will absolutely enjoy unforgettable glimpses of the city.

**The Sacre-Coeur**
The Catholic Basilica, built between 1875 and 1914, rises on top of Montmartre hill and overlooks the district with its bulk and the glittering white of its stones.

There are plenty of gourmet and convivial opportunities in Paris: **wine bars, cafés, bistros...**

## "I like Montmartre's bakeries, cafés and bars."

Lelouch knows how to look at the city, magically. Its beauty reveals and belongs to another dimension: "I like discovering Paris from the water. I believe the *bateau-mouche*, though touristic, still remains a very romantic way to get close to this city and fall in love with it. The Seine flows gently among old-time spectacular monuments and buildings, guardians of lots and lots of people's stories", he thinks.

"Where do I like going walking? I walk in Montmartre and watch people, the crowd. I often walk around the Bois de Boulogne, when I need to think, write...", he admits that's the place inspires him most. "I write my films while I am walking, jotting down notes on my phone...." That's how some of his masterpieces were born. Between two instants of Paris charming attraction.

**The Musée d'Orsay**
Sailing on a *bateau-mouche* you can admire the Musée d'Orsay fa-cade. Once a train sta-tion, the building was restored by the architect Gae Aulenti. Currently it hosts a rich French art collection dating back to 1848–1914.

# MISS TIC

## The Queen of Street Art

Long dark hair, falling wavy on her shoulders, as if she was a mermaid. Intense and mysterious eyes, evidenced by her long eyelashes. A small tattoo on her shoulder, with her name on. While watching her, as beautiful as a diva, you seem to recognize her in some of the women she paints on Paris walls...

Like poetic muses, echoing her thoughts, turning them into phrases you can read on the walls: "C'est la vie, ça va passer" (That's life, it will pass) "Pret-à-porter" (easy to wear, easy to carry), with a female figure carrying a man on her shoulders... "Alerte à la bombe. ART ROCK"... (Beware of the bomb. ART ROCK), and also "Je cherche la vérité et un appartement" (I seek the truth and an apartment), "Plus fort que la passion, l'illusion" (Illusion, stronger than passion)... Every time her works are not only an aesthetic masterpiece, but also evoke reflections, emotions, they strike the heart. They mix together glamour and poetry, phrases and refined or ironic texts, colors and sensual, charming shapes, sometimes provocative, with feminine body flights and fractions. Like a magic spell. Miss Tic is the "Street Art Queen" and in 2015 she celebrated thirty years of her career in Lélia Mordoch's gallery, with a retrospective developing a "future looking back at memory" throughout revised and reinter-

> I wanted to leave my name in Paris memories. I plunged my claws on this city walls.

preted works. Her art represents Paris artistic essence. She has worked here since 1985, inspiring the more and more fashionable urban art collecting, since then.

"I wanted to leave my name in Paris memories. I plunged my claws on this city walls. I offered myself to the most beautiful art gallery of the world. My works address to everybody and for thirty years my creations have beaten the daily rhythm of thousands of people", she confesses with regards to her relationship with the city.

How do you get inspired in your artistic work? "I breathe Paris, it gives me inspiration. I really taste it, it seizes me completely. I look at Paris, she recognizes me, I breathe the smell of Paris, with Yves Saint Laurent Rive Gauche, I write on Paris, I'm very close to it."

Miss Tic was born in Paris, Montmartre, on 20th February 1956, from a father of Tunisian origins and a mother from Normandy. Her street painting started to take shape among the roads and alleys she was born, where she spent part of her childhood. Her family moved to Orly, indeed. She lost her mother when she was ten, her younger brother in a car accident, and her father when she was sixteen. She was raised by her step-mother and in the 80s she lived in California for a while.

Irony, sensuality, poetry, femininity: these are just some of Miss Tic's **street art** features.

Then she came back to Paris, as she missed it too much and wanted to change her life. She started to experiment beyond Montmartre, in Ménilmontant, the Marais, Montorgueil and the Butte-aux-Cailles.

Paris is in her blood, it vibrates and lights up her soul. Montmartre is now a tourist district and has always been artists' homeland. In the 60s and 70s it was featured by a lively proletarian and working class street life, with prostitutes and ordinary criminal actions. Its memory is pop, highly passionate and sensual, bohemian, fetishist, erotic, wonderful in all its contrasts, colored in different cultures and ethnic groups living together side by side. These are all elements standing out in Miss Tic works. Her al-

ways very attractive women, have curvy bodies evoking sensual desire. They catch the eye and bewitch, never leave indifferent, in spite of the metropolis vibrant rhythm: they pop out of a wall, at a shop or a café window, they wink at the corner of a street...

"I was born in Paris. I have a passionate relationship with this city. I live here and it's my shelter. It's in my skin. I'm a true Parisian! Sometimes I leave the city and I find it even more enchanting when I come back", she confides, while she tells where she spreads her art.

How do you choose the places for your works? "When I paint on walls, I chose the districts I know, I don't like feeling a stranger. I select the walls according to their look, materials and lights.

Miss Tic's work on a wall of **avenue Ledru-Rollin.**

**Social themes** come out of Miss Tic's work displayed on a wall in rue de Paradis.

I paint at eye level. I find myself alone facing a wall, and after that I melt together with others, thanks to the power of poetry", she says.

Miss Tic's works have been spared from the passing of time and their possible disappearance, and exhibited in art galleries, transported on canvas, tore down the walls, concrete parts and other materials like steel plates, plastic surfaces, wood and collage. "I have exhibited for thirty years in art galleries; art dealers choose the artists they want to make known. I'm represented by two Parisian galleries: The Lélia Mordoch gallery in rue Mazarine and the

Brugier-Rigail gallery in rue Volta. I approach visual art like a poet. I don't want to withdraw, neither externally nor internally. I like contamination between private and public. Everything starts in my art studio, my works change whether they are editions, exhibitions or urban space", she points out. "Galleries are a way not to be shut in street art, to exist with art market actors, as well: savoir-faire (traditional craftwork ability) and faire-savoir (informing)."

Her women, her men have also bewitched fashion and were used even by Louis Vuitton, Kenzo, Longchamp. In 2007, Miss Tic has also

"When I paint on walls,
I chose the districts I know,
I don't like feeling a stranger.
I select the walls according to
their look, materials
and lights."

been chosen by Claude Chabrol to illustrate the film poster "A Girl Cut In Two."

Where does your inspiration come from? "From life." And what advice would you give to an artist in Paris? "I would suggest him to soak in, to be led by the city. To get all chances, to listen to each sound and silence of this city. He will soon discover its music, its poetry, the beauty of a rich in history and humanity urban site continually evolving."

Her relation with Paris is strictly connected to places and times giving emotions, but also to the past and to many other artists who have lived or currently live here. "I like walking, strolling along the streets, at day-time or at night. I am always moved by thinking of poets, philosophers, artists who were here before me. At times I feel I'm about to bump into Oscar Wilde in rue des Beaus Arts or Edith Piaf in Belleville. Or to glimpse Henry Miller at Place de Clichy and Colette in Palais Royal gardens. And then my colleagues I come across for real, like Lydie Salvayre in all her beauty in rue de Charonne, Agnès Varda in rue Daguerre or Jacques Villeglé in an alley of the Marais district", she explains. What do you like best of your city? I love Paris cafés and terraces.

**Montmartre** shields the bohemian atmosphere that has marked Miss Tic's artistic beginning. Currently it's an extremely popular tourist destination.

Here I drink Martini with my friends, we comment, gossip, make fun or wonder about people and passers-by. I have lots of memories of terraces, like Le Dôme, in rue Montparnasse where I used to meet Raymond Hains right in front of Le Sélect terrace. Here, Jean Baudrillard used to buy me coffee."

What are your special places? "I strongly recommend Le Mazarin and Le Balto, in rue Mazarine for a fun aperitif with artists, gallerists and art lovers. In the 10th arrondissement, I savor the best pizzas at I Cugini, 33 rue du Paradis. I also show my friends small museums I'm fond of: the Musée de la Vie Romantique (the Museum of Romantic life), the Musée Zadkine and the Musée Gustave Moreau."

The French Capital offers hints to enchanting walks... "I like the Jardin de Luxembourg, with photo exhibitions along the gates and a pond where generations of children have sailed their wooden boats. There is also a bowling and a chess area, some kiosks with musicians, some tai chi practice areas, orchid and begonia greenhouses and visitors from all over the world", she says. "And I obviously love the Seine and the embankment on both sides... Crossing Paris along the Seine, I've always been struck by the banks recognized by Unesco as worldwide heritage. But I like strolling along them far from the Paris-Plage chaos and anxiety!"

Where to walk best in this no boundary metropolis? "Everywhere. From South to North, from East to West. From the Goutte d'Or to Pigalle, from the Butte aux Cailles to the Butte Montmartre. From the Chinese district in the 13th arrondissement to the Indian one in the 10th. In the most bohemian districts of the

**Urban Landscapes**
Lamark-Caulaincourt metro station, at the foot of Montmartre hill, takes on a peculiar atmosphere in the evening.

**The Maison Rose**
The Maison Rose bistro in Montmartre appears in one of Maurice Utrillo's paintings. He was born in Montmartre in 1883.

Some of Paris symbols are towering and iconic, as well as lightened and rich in history: the July Column in **place de la Bastille** (on the left) commemorates the Revolution.

Marais and Saint-Germain-des-Prés. From République to Bastille. From place Denfert-Rochereau to place de la Nation. Just to find yourself in place de la Concorde at 6 a.m. or enjoying the sunset from Passerelle des Arts... I get crazy about urban deviations."

Thinking about a suitable color to represent Paris, Miss Tic states: "It would be an endless range of gray and there are far more than 50 shades of gray... in Paris. All the world dreams of discovering Paris. It's a cosmopolitan city where all nationalities, religions, ethnic groups and various cultures mix up. That's Paris strength, its integrating power, despite all the differences."

She is always sure that Paris will continue its full arts Renaissance. "This city has passed through centuries, wars, revolutions, festivals, attacks, chaos, curfews, celebrations... History continues and evolves...", she states. And she herself is ready for new adventures: "I've just published the book 'FLASHBACK, 30 years of creation', and I have displayed a small exhibition in Paris, in Lélia Mordoch's gallery. To underline that no one is a prophet in his own land, I will be part of the exhibited artists at Berthéas gallery - not in Paris but in Vichy - for a great retrospective of my 30 years of creation, with about a hundred works! Therefore with great joy and enthusiasm I'm getting ready for this huge event, but also with some sadness and bitterness thinking that the city I've dedicated the best of my artistic creation doesn't open any door in its cultural institutions...." This is Paris but you cannot stop loving it, after all.

# DOMINIQUE PERRAULT
## The Innovator

Dynamic images woven into social and cultural values, hints taken from minimalism and conceptual arts aiming at enriching shapes and structures. An open and flexible approach tending to accept uncertainties but denying modern architecture dogmatism, in relationship with the surrounding landscape. Glass and metal production, glass walls revealing through the intensification of the light rather than their structure. They seem inspired by contemporary technology without being restricted. The innovation succeeds beyond the barely engineering level.

Dominique Perrault is one of the best architects and city planners of our times. His view wavers between Rationalism and Structuralism, though internationally unique, and marks history. He dares the progress... "Paris fell asleep after François Mitterand. He worked out great projects awarding France exceptional beauty. Today we are seeing Paris awakening throughout its districts life and the development of forthcoming projects. Paris is currently a constellation of small projects. Hence it's getting better and better" he argues referring to his city which has become his creative laboratory, his muse and source of inspiration for many projects and new ideas.

> My vision of Paris is the establishment of a relation between Heritage and Modernity.

Perrault was born in Clermont-Ferrand in 1953. He has a vivid memory of his first approach with the French capital. A predictive memory about his artistic future. "When I was a kid, my father brought me to Paris to buy my first bike, in avenue de la Grande Armée, at Peugeot stores. It was a typical blue Peugeot bike. I remember that big shop window, the building... It was the time of Alain Delon and Mireille Darc" he reminds with a vein of melancholy but still positive.

"This Peugeot building has then become one of my agency projects, of course! We are working on its restoration and renovation" he adds.

Perrault was so inspired by Paris from the start that he decided to study here. He graduated in architecture at the Ecole Nationale Supérieure des Beaux-Arts, in 1978, and then he achieved a qualification in city planning at the Ecole Supérieure des Ponts et Chaussée, and in history at the Ecole 3des Hautes Etudes en Sciences Sociales.

His career followed its course strictly connected to the city. "When I was studying architecture at the Beaux-Arts de Paris, I lived in a 'chambre de bonne', as we call the old servant rooms, in place Dauphine, Île de la Cité.

**Rue Dauphine** (on the left) shapes a perspective together with the square bearing the same name on the île de la Cité. They are connected by **Pont Neuf** (on the right).

"When I was studying architecture at the Beaux-Arts de Paris, I lived in a chambre de bonne in place Dauphine."

Soon after I started my first job at Paris municipality, as a city planner of the Atelier Parisien d'urbanisme (APUR). I followed a consistently Parisian path. From place Dauphine, to rue Bonaparte, to the Hôtel de Ville, the Town Hall and the Bibliothèque Nationale de France, favoring the enhancement of the 13th arrondissement big district. In accordance with the historical heritage, we are restoring the Poste du Louvre, in the city centre. This is a third Republic monument, an industrial hub meant to became an urban space, for a range of uses. It's opened to the metropolis, its in-

habitants and its visitors... a unique experience since this building will be operative twenty-four hours, any time, day and night" he says, letting thoughts flow towards the future but keeping them attached to memory.

Perrault opened his studio in the French capital in 1981, working out his own style right from the start. Here he carried out the work that made him stand out in the history of architecture: the Bibliothèque Nationale de France, in 1989. A library which shape reminds of a series of open books, standing around a central courtyard. He accomplished many other works.

**Place de l'Hôtel de Ville**, Paris city hall. Currently also known as Esplanade de la Libération.

Among them: the Velodrom, the Berlin Olympic Pool, the enlargement of the Court of Justice of the European Union in Luxembourg, the Olympic Tennis Stadium in Madrid, the insurance company Fukoku ana Osaka tower, the EWHA, Women's University in Seoul, the restoration of Piazza Garibaldi in Naples; and he built the highest skyscrapers of Vienna, the DC Towers. His projects are exhibited all over the world and a great exhibition was planned in his honor, at the Centre Georges Pompidou in Paris. He also led renovation projects like at the Longchamp race-course, and, as he reminds, at the Poste du Louvre, both in Paris, and at Dufour Pavilion in Versailles. His work is described as following the great tradition of the French geometrical monumentality, with his urbanism treating nature as voluntary geography. And he has brought himself to the edges of "Arte Povera". Among his "creatures" in Paris, there are: the industrial building of the "Hôtel Industriel Jean-Baptiste Berlier", the big greenhouse for the Cité

**Allegory of the Arts**
The main entrance of the Hôtel de Ville is flanked by two allegorical bronze statues: Arts and Science. The Arts one was sculpted by Laurent Marqueste in 1882.

des Sciences et de l'Industrie, the parking-garage Emile Durkheim, the B&B Hotel, the Sammode offices, the BnF MK2, the commercial development of the National Library for its François Mitterrand side, the Villejuif IGR/Grand Paris Express station. And, when asked about about his favorite monument, he says: "Definitively the Mémorial des Martyrs de la Déportation, planned by the architect Georges-Henri Pingusson, in 1962. It's placed on the Eastern corner of the Île de la Cité, the heart of Paris, and it offers a beautiful view on the apse of Notre-Dame Cathedral", he explains, probably referring to another master of architecture who may have influenced him somehow. "If I think about a drawing for this city? I would say the 2024 Olympic Games Paris", he predicts, wishing for his future city.

Perrault's work was awarded many recognitions. Among them: the Grand Prix National d'Architecture in 1993, the Mies Van Der Rohe Prize in 1997, the golden medal by the French Academy of Architecture in 2010 and the Praemium Imperiale Laureate for architecture in 2015. Currently he's directing the Dominique Perrault Architecture (DPA) studio and he is involved in several activities. He's a professor at the

**BNF**
The four angular towers of the Bibliothèque National de France were designed by Perrault. They recall the shape of open books and each has a name: time, law, numbers and literature.

Polytechnique Fédérale de Lausanne and has been a member of the Conseil Scientifique de l'Atelier International du Grand Paris, since 2012. In 2013, Bucharest University of Architecture and Urbanism appointed him "Doctor Honoris Causa".

Perrault finds important to regain his human dimension in Paris, though his many recognitions all over the world. "I live and work in the 11th arrondissement, in a former 2000 square meter factory, with a considerable difference in volumes and a big hall. It's placed in Paul Bert district. It's like three districts in one, with some dominant features: it is of Jewish origins and traditions, popular and bobo at the same time" he says, with the enthusiasm of rediscovering love for the most intimate part of his city.

"When you take rue Léon Frot, you find out a a pattern of nice small adjacent streets not cleaned up or set apart yet, considering urban renewal and the dwellers'occupation. Here children play, people chat out of their houses and there's still some vegetation on the walls... They represent daily life moments, something that keeps local ordinary life intact" he goes on, revealing unexpected details of his district.

**Mémorial Des Martyrs De La Déportation**
It was inaugurated in 1962, in memory of all those who were deported to the Nazis concentration camps during World War II.

"My favorite monument is the Mémorial des Martyrs
de la Déportation. Placed on the Eastern corner of the Île de la Cité,
the heart of Paris, it offers a beautiful view on the apse
of Notre-Dame Cathedral."

The **Mémorial de la Shoah**, in the Marais district, was inaugurated in 2005. It includes a museum, a documentation center
and several places of remembrance, like the tomb of the unknown Jewish soldier.

"In Paris we are seeing a renovation of cafés and 'bistronomie', bistros creative cuisine."

The **Ecailler du Bistrot** is one of Perrault's favorite location, placed at 22 rue Paul Bert, in the 11th arrondissement. It proposes a fish-based menu and the furniture is in tune with the food. It is enriched with old boats models, bottles full of sand and sea themed paintings.

**Paris roofs**, with their gray hues are a common feature of the urban landscape, whether they belong to the Louvre (on the right) or to one among the many stately homes in the city center.

He's very familiar with some places in Paris, of course. "I recommend the Écailler du bistrot, it's awesome! The cuisine is based on fish and seafood and they will open oysters in front of you. They are among the tastiest and easiest to make dishes. For a still young man like me it's perfect! But there is Paul Bert, as well. A meat products bistro run by a 'slowfood King'!" he says, referring to Paris gastronomy extraordinariness.

Is Paris changing? "There are two changing levels in this city" he clarifies. "On a local level we can see a growing proximity identity in the districts: the so called 'Paris aux cents villages', Paris with a hundred villages. On one side there are more and more shops, organic food shops, the AMAP (association pour le maintien d'une agriculture paysanne), on the other we

are seeing a renovation of cafés and 'bistrono-mie', bistros creative cuisine. On a global scale, a change is developing in the Grand Paris, with its 12 million inhabitants on a 50km area" he goes on. While he's gathering reflections of life, he reminds the past. "Twenty years ago, you could drive everywhere in Paris. Now it's totally different! I've got an Old Timer, a vintage car. I prefer getting a taxi, or better walking. It's wonderful to walk in Paris. It's a real 'ville de promenade', a city for walks!" he reveals speaking of how he likes wandering about, in this beautiful metropolis.

How do you see the city in your fancy? "Paris is fifty shades of gray, of metal roofs... A darker and a lighter gray" he believes transfiguring it like an image right in front of his eyes.

"Today we are seeing Paris awakening throughout
its districts life and the development of forthcoming projects.
Paris is currently a constellation of small projects.
Hence it's getting better and better."

Perrault's view of future Paris: a rendering of **place de l'Etoile** with the Arc de Triomphe.

As a great city planner he passionately wishes for his big ideal planning. "I see Paris in the future like a city with no outskirts boulevard. It chokes the city. Grand Paris development will enable to assimilate all the areas within a unique metropolis. It starts with gathering the transport networks and the stations like Grand Paris Express Villejuif-IGR, planned on the south of Paris. Paris future is beyond Paris", he believes.

Perrault doesn't simply own a simplistic idea, just like his architecture. "My vision of Paris is the establishment of a relation between Heritage and Modernity. In my studio we carried out so-called 'fictions' like the Arc de Triomphe place de l'Etoile. They are imaginary proposals for Grand Paris, an argumentative and explanatory vocation, as within French great architectural utopias. The strategy that we apply on the Arc de Triomphe, consists of facing the metropolis and its heritage by working on its root structure. The Arc de Triomphe so becomes the symbol of Paris revelation" he admits describing utopia that can become reality. In the end, no place like Paris is capable of surprising and recreating any moment of artistic expression.

The **Poste du Louvre** restructuring project that Perrault's architecture firm is working at, combines a view of the future with an acknowledgment of the past.

# MARIE-CLAUDE PIETRAGALLA

## The Dance Icon

Pure femininity expressing in a movement, a gesture, her look with the crescendo of music and her legs following gently and determinately. Her bewitching and irresistible grace, still strong and passionate. A vision touching society and art, transfiguring emotion, making it as beautiful as truth, able to deeply touch the heart, shake souls, make you think, fall in love with her incredible and extraordinary creative vein. The dancer and choreographer Marie-Claude Pietragalla is Paris and France dance icon, a myth to the entire world. She managed to distinguish herself by shaping her own, unique style. She loves experimenting, facing new challenges, questioning rather than providing answers.

**Paris keeps reshaping itself, attached to its identity, its beauty and its thirst craving for freedom.**

As a true artist, she needs to evoke answers expressing the talent and ideas she gets from everything surrounding her, people and life moments. As for her city: "Paris will always be Paris, the most beautiful city of the world", Maurice Chevalier used to sing. "The French capital, with its cultural heritage, history and dynamism, keeps reshaping itself, attached to its identity, its beauty and its thirst craving for freedom", Marie-Claude states.

Her eyes are intense dark, they may explore your soul, going deep to reach an infinite nuances of expressions, revealing in dancing, as if she was able to shape humanity in all its aspects. Creativity in its own purity matters most, she thinks, after all.

She was born on 2nd February 1963. She has always had fire in her blood... She admits she was an exuberant girl and she was attracted by martial arts. Her mother enrolled her in dance classes. Right soon, she understood she wanted to enter the Opéra de Paris, even though she couldn't figure out the environment. But she was determined. When she was nine, she got into the Opéra school dance. She had already established herself with her own talent, standing out among her colleagues and entering the corps de ballet. When she was twenty-five, she was titled *prima ballerina* and after two years *étoile*. But she felt her vocation would have led her further on... Marie-Claude has always stated that she doesn't feel just like a dancer, but a "dancing woman": the human being, so full of sensitivity and instinct, is at the core of her perception. She approaches her audience in that way.

"I love the paved alleys of Montmartre with its fabric market, the Père Lachaise cemetery, the hôtels particuliers."

She believes that dance shouldn't be elite art, but accessible to and understandable by everybody, up to the point of reaching a wide and articulated audience. Her inspiration distinguishes her from any other dancer and links her with her truly Parisian nature, which has enchanted many other artists through the years never letting them go...

The French capital fascinated her right from the start. The same creative vein conveying in Marie-Claude's restless soul. "I was born in Paris. I discovered it since I was very young. I used to soak myself in its energy, strength, beauty", she says. When she thinks of when she was a girl, her memories run to exquisite thoughts: "My childhood memories are made of suspended moments, colorful dreams, walks in tune with fantasy and unconsciousness", she reveals.

**Place du Tertre**
The picturesque square on top of Montmartre hill is attended by painters, artists and caricaturists livening it up anytime.

213

There is a great artistic and mastery work behind each play at the **Comédie Française**.

On opposite Seine banks, the **théâtre du Châtelet** (on the right) and the **Conciergerie** palace, on the île de la Cité.

# JOËL ROBUCHON
## The Cuisine Master

Perfection, innovation, fantasy. These ones seem to be the fundamental ingredients of his culinary art. Joël Robuchon is considered the absolute master of gastronomy, appointed chef of the century, he boasts most Michelin stars in the world. He's also acknowledged the most influent French chef of post-nouvelle cuisine of this time. Cooking is like a vision for Robuchon, like the one of a great Renaissance artist: he doesn't only imagine a dish, but also creates new perspectives, refined ways to approach the pleasure of food. He hasn't only won Paris, but also all the planet corners where he opened several restaurants, as well as experts', culinary critics' and celebrities' refined taste. He thinks there is the perfect dish, the unreachable one, the one that can always be better, the one you will never stop looking for and trying, again and again. He got influenced by the authentic French cuisine, the so-called bourgeois cuisine, getting away from the most diversified nouvelle cuisine and its extremes but coming closer to the Eastern one. In 1976 he was titled "Meilleur Ouvrier de France", in 1987 "Chef de l'année", in 1990 "Cuisinier du siècle" and he keeps experimenting, looking ahead to the future.

"I love Paris all, a city out of ordinary with its blend of traditions and modernism, culture, architecture, shopping, markets, small shops, bakeries, cheese shops, butcheries, bistros, French gastronomy... let alone its arrogance, traffic jams and wild parking...", he states. And he thinks back to his career, his success, his numerous books (among them: *Simply French, Tout Robuchon, French Cheeses, Joël Robuchon Cooking Through the Seasons, La Cuisine de Joël Robuchon, L'Atelier of Joël Robuchon: The Artistry of a Master Chef and His Protégés, Le Grand Larousse Gastronomique, Food and Life, Joël Robuchon and Dr. Nadia Volf)*, his TV shows, but first and foremost his memories, his dearest treasure.

Paris is an entire part of his memory. The relationship with his city is lost in the mists of time and is strictly related to his creativity. He was born on 7th April 1945 in Poitiers. At the beginning he thought he would become a seminarist, but Paris enchanted him with its numberless spells... "As a young man from Poitiers, I discovered Paris when I was fourteen: its boulevards, outskirts, historic bridges, monuments – a pleasure of architecture – I used to cycle along them... I know the roads maybe better than the majority of the taxi drivers", he remembers.

> I discovered Paris when I was fourteen: its boulevards, outskirts, historic bridges, monuments – a pleasure of architecture – I used to cycle along them.

"In my laboratory in Paris I work out the recipes
I serve in about the twenty restaurants I run all over the world.
Here I prepare all my menus."

The **Atelier Etoile de Joël Robuchon** restaurant, on the Champs-Élysées is the second restaurant the chef opened in Paris.

The **Atelier Saint-Germain de Joël Robuchon** restaurant was appointed one of the 12 best restaurants in the world,
by a specialized magazine in 2012.

"My first wonder was discovering the Eiffel Tower, the French capital icon", he adds referring to the most intense impression he had from the first impact with the city.

He started his cuisine adventure in Paris, as an apprentice, up to become claimed chef. "I had the pleasure to debut in Paris as a chef at the Auberge du Vert-Galant, l'Île de la Cité, Paris ancient cradle, at the Clos des Bernardins in rue de Pontoise, near the Notre-Dame Cathedral, at Le Berkeley in avenue Matignon, on the barge Île-de-France along Avenue Kennedy, before working at the hotel Concorde La Fayette of Porte Mailot, at the hotel Nikko of quai de Grenell and at the Jamin in rue de Longchamp, near Trocadero. He has a clientele including celebrities and stars that only Paris, la Ville Lumière could offer", he underlines, referring to the many chances this metropolis gives. A charm like the one of a seductive woman making people fall in love and hard to resist.

Joël achieved the direction of the Concorde Lafayette Hotel cuisine when he was 29, leading 90 chefs and serving thousands of courses per day. His reliability, strictness, professionalism and high talent made him gain a great reputation from the very start. As a chef at the Nikko hotel, he got two Michelin stars and, in 1981, opened

**Oysters** are a Northern France specialty, as well as an important term of local economy and a strong call for gourmet lovers.

> "I love Paris all, its markets, small shops, bakeries, cheese shops, butcheries, bistros, French gastronomy."

the Jamin restaurant, where he was given the maximum recognition, the three Michelin stars and a success that hasn't stopped.

Robuchon learned from Paris how to deeply impress. Just like when, after seven years of voluntary "culinary exile", due to health problems or maybe just because he wanted to have a break, with the intention of retiring when he was fifty, he opened the Atelier Saint-Germain in rue Montalembert, in Paris: it's the first restaurant with no tables, where you can sit at a bar, only separated by a thin divider inviting you to socialize in a convivial flair like in a contemporary Renaissance banquet. A concept then expanded with the Atelier Etoile, at the Champs Élysées.

Robuchon is an artist who can dare and stand comparison. So his kitchens are open, their furniture is elegant and minimal, like his choice of ingredients: since just the sublime one can cook delicious dishes able to bewitch the palate with the bare minimum. His dishes don't often include more than three ingredients.

Following the principle

**Food markets**
The Marché Beauvau opened in 1843 and is placed in the 12th arrondissement. It's a covered market where you can find an excellent choice of meat, fish, cheese, fruit and vegetables.

of making his cuisine accessible to everybody, for more than ten years Robuchon has hosted the TV show Bon Appetit Bien Sûr, with Guy Job, a daily appointment offering practical cuisine lessons and introducing one chef each week teaching easy and cheap recipes and providing tips and tricks. Since 2011 Robuchon he has hold the Planète Gourmande show, where he used to give gourmet hints. You can find all his products, as first-class wines, in his shop at 3 rue Paul-Louis Courier.

Joël has always traveled around the world, visiting Japan on a regular basis to discover new products and learn Eastern techniques he's passionate about. He also got enthusiast about tapas Spanish bars. But Paris remains deeply-rooted in his soul. Here stays his creative cuisine: "In my laboratory in Paris I work out the recipes I serve in about the twenty restaurants I run all over the world. Here I prepare all my menus." According to him, the French capital remains the most magic city. It inspires him to create gastronomy spells then traveling and bewitching all the world, in his restaurants in Bordeaux, Bangkok, Tokyo, London, Munich, Macao, Hong Kong, Las Vegas, Taipei, Singapore, New York, Shangai, Montreal, Mumbai, Geneva, Miami.

**The Boucherie**
Among Parisian butchers there is who still speaks the "Louchébem" slang, dating back to the 19th century.

**À la Mere de Famille**
Montmartre old sweet-shop and chocolaterie was founded in 1761 and is currently a listed building.

RUE DU
FAUBOURG
MONTMARTRE

A LA MÈRE DE FAMILLE

FRUITS

SECS

FRUITS

CONFITS

CHOCOLATS

THÉS

A **bouquiniste** kiosk selling second-hand books, old newspapers and old-time Paris prints.

Nearby the Pont d'Iéna, it's quite common to bump into some artists exhibiting their works, along the **Seine banks**.

## "I love walking along the Seine banks, it's stimulating."

What's the secret to be a restaurant owner and a chef in Paris? "You can't cook good food if you don't love people and the Parisians are charming and often gourmets. Adjusting to the Parisians and their current style life is fundamental", he points out, describing what distinguishes French people living in Paris. "The Parisians are casual, fashionable and attached to national values. They want to celebrate special occasions, work commitments, birthdays and anniversaries... in a gourmet restaurant. At lunch they rush, instead. They enjoy bistros and the Atelier Etoile, a welcoming, chilled, cosmo-

politan place. Here they can taste French cuisine made of classical and modern dishes", he goes on. "What's a typical dish outlining Paris best? A tasty baguette", he says thinking about what best reflects the local and popular culinary soul!

"My favorite district is where I live: the Eiffel Tower one, the 15th arrondissement. It's central, quite close to every place, convivial, with

**The Bateau-mouche**
At the foot of the Seine banks, or sitting on board of a boat crossing the river, Paris reveals its essence and its hidden sides.

many shops, refined bars and products like cheese, bakeries, early fruit and vegetables, butchers, groceries, the Centre Beuagrenelle. I love its social mixing and variety", he admits showing to be attached to the places defining his everyday life. "One of my favorite restaurants is La Stresa, in rue Chambiges. Its typical Italian cuisine, its warm and familiar atmosphere, ensured by Fabiola brothers", he says.

Robuchon is sure that the city will keep intact its multi-ethnic soul making it unique and fascinating because made up of different cultures and traditions living together like a magic whole. Even gastronomic... "Paris stays a key city for worldwide cuisine. The majority of the international chefs have learned here their own profession", he points out.

His inspiration keeps developing in this incredible and unique city. "I love walking along the Seine banks, it's stimulating...", he suggests. Thinking about a color defining Paris... Blue, white and red... And a smell? Fresh bread and cakes", he concludes, thinking you can often smell it in the air, in a contagious flair, warming the heart. And Robuchon is fond of it.

**Enlightened history**
The city historic phases reflect in its monuments: from the Middle-Ages to the Revolution, from the Napoleonic time to the Belle Epoque.

The **National Assembly**, French Parliament leading branch, is placed in the Neoclassical Palais Bourbon.

# ELIE SAAB
## The Dressmaking Wizard

Vocation is in his blood like a primordial instinct, a healthy obsession leading him to invent, create, get inspired. He has owned it since he was born, when he wasn't aware of it and then it has grown inside. Elie Saab: one of the most important *couturière*, appreciated by cinema divas and high society ladies.

He has always been passionate about dressmaking, sharp with needle and thread, up to the point of starting making her sister's dresses when he was nine. When he was a boy, he used to sell his dresses to the women of his district, since his willingness and his ideas urged him to aim at perfect art with no boundaries. His Lebanese talent was vibrating in his veins and it would lead him far ahead... to discover the world, and to Paris. "Paris, the *Haute Couture* capital, has always been my dream. As far as I can go back to my memories, I've always known I would establish my brand there, one day. Launching my collection in this city marked my start within the international fashion industry. Since then, Paris has become my second home", he says.

As far as I can go back to my memories, I've always known I would establish my brand, one day, in the Ville Lumière.

Right from the start, his clothes have stood out due to their refinement and femininity, care for details, embroidery, pearls, and soft fabrics shaping bodies sinuously. His fashion mixes up fantasy and grandeur, a style in love with women, enhancing their elegance, their sensuality, making them appealing, enchanting, unforgettable. "When I first visited Paris, I confirmed my ambition of settling and displaying my collections here. My picture became clear and I issued the challenge", Saab admits.

Elie Saab was born in 1964 in Damour, Lebanon. He's self-taught and approached dressmaking animated by a strong passion. In 1982, he founded his atelier in Beirut, already well aware of all the secrets of his profession that he had acquired during his childhood. His unlimited and exclusive style was already shining bright. In the same year he showed his first collection at the Casino du Liban, gaining immediate success, up to get worldwide attention as well as high society's one. In 1986, Saab met his wife Claudine and they had three children. Elie Jr., Selim and Michel.

Around 1996, his clothes started catwalking, thanks to the celebrities who appreciated the intimate elegance of his style.

In 1997, Saab was invited to the prestigious National Chamber of Italian Fashion. He was the first foreign fashion designer becoming a member of it and he had showed his *Haute Couture* collections for three years, together with gaining a resounding success at the Fashion Week in Milan, in 1998. The Whole world great fashion stores started to buy his collection and Queen Rania of Jordan fell so much in love with his clothes, that she commissioned him her coronation dress, in 1999.

In Paris, in 2002, he launched his first *Haute Couture* collection and in 2002 he became a member of the Chambre Syndicale de la Haute Couture. Since then he has kept planning two *Haute Couture* collections per year.

"I adore Paris. Its rich culture is definitively the source of my inspiration. I can get inspired by everything surrounding me, in Paris. It may be the architecture of an important monument, an atmosphere, a painting, a sculpture... I like wandering and watching the Parisians in their daily life", he says, thinking of the most irresistible element in the French capital. "French women are a source of my

**The Fontaine des Fleuves**
Inaugurated in 1840, the fountain in place de la Concorde, together with its companion representing the seas, used to celebrate France naval power.

*"When I walk in Paris, I like venturing around Place des Vosges, in the Marais district and visiting the amazing art galleries along rue de Seine, in the 6th arrondissement."*

inspiration, as well. I love how they manage to blend light heartedness and simplicity. They're elegant with no effort", he comments, revealing a special sensitivity towards femininity in all its aspects, in its soul as well as in sheer superficiality.

His fame has incessantly grown since 2002, when the American actress Halle Berry chose to wear his dress on the night of the Academy Awards. She was the first black leading actress winning the Oscar with the film "Monster's Ball". In the same year, Saab opened his first salon Haute Couture in the distinguished 8th arrondissement, satisfying his more and more cosmopolitan customers. In 2003, the President of the Lebanese Republic awarded him the honor of the Ordre National du Cèdre, while in 2005, Saab inaugurated a five floor building in Beirut and launched his first *Prêt-à-porter* collection in Paris, together with an accessories one. The following year, Saab was included at the Chambre Syndicale de la Haute Couture as a "membre correspondant".

**The Musée Galliera**
Inaugurated in 1977, the Musée de la Mode de la Ville de Paris is hosted in a 19th century palace that used to belong to Duchess Galliera.

**Protection and Future**
The neo Reinassance Palais Galliera hosts some classical statues, like the one sculpted by Honoré Icard in 1893.

In 2007, he confirmed his choice of Paris as his second home opening a new Haute Couture salon and his brand shop, respectively at 1 rond-point des Champs-Élysées and at 43 avenue Franklin Roosevelt.

Over the years, Saab has opened his boutiques in London, Dubai, Hong Kong, Mexico City and Moscow. In 2009 he launched a fragrance and Beauté Prestige International beauty products. His first perfume was Elie Saab Le Parfum. Others followed, up to the most recent Rose Couture. In 2012 Countess Stephanie de Lannoy married the Prince of Luxembourg and she wore one of Saab's dress. Many other noble people chose his clothes for the ceremony. At the end of 2012, Saab moved to Paris.

**Rue de Seine**
This street in the 6th arrondissement, well known for its art galleries and antiques boutiques, has some modernity features, like street art.

A contemporary art gallery displays works in **rue de Seine**, where important fashion brand buildings can be found.

Placed in avenue George V, the so called Golden Triangle, **Elie Saab**'s second **Parisian boutique** shows the fashion designer's clothes and accessories.

"I adore Paris. Its rich culture is definitively the source of my inspiration. I can get inspired by everything surrounding me."

"My favorite district? I love the 16th arrondissement where I founded my Parisian headquarter, in avenue Raymond Poincaré. I also like Palais Galliera district and avenue Pierre 1er de Serbie district", he reveals. His headquarter is in an 18th century building, with a typical Parisian architecture: parquet floor, marble stairs, old mirrors and big chandeliers. His offices are modern, featured by a luxury minimalism, and reflect the great fashion designer's style, his clean and contemporary lines.

Saab introduced a "Poincaré" bag line carried out in his Parisian study, for 2014-2015 Autumn-Winter collection.

Saab believes Parisian hotels are fascinating: "I favor the Four Seasons George V Hotel, standing on eight floors, with an important art collection and a perfect location in the heart of the Golden Triangle.

I opened my second Parisian boutique right near this hotel, in 2015", he underlines. In November 2015, he worked out his "shop-in-shop" idea in the Le Printemps Haussmann stores. Like many artists, he likes getting lost in the city, chasing inspiration. "When I walk in Paris, I like venturing around Place des Vosges, Le Marais district and visiting the amazing art galleries along rue de Seine, in the 6th arrondissement", he explains.

He carried out lots of projects in Paris: a dual format volume was published in 2003. It covers the history of his fashion industry displaying his evolution as a man and as an artist; in 2004 he launched his monthly magazine "The Light of Now", about fashion, design, art, music and perfumes. In Spring 2016 he worked out his new bag line, "le 31", and established a partnership with Safilo for a glasses line.

**Place des Vosges**
Originally called Place Royale, in 1800 Marais square was rebaptized with its current name in honor of the Vosges the first department paying taxes to the revolutionary Government.

Paris provides hints, suggestions, and ideas to such a creative fashion designer,

"If I wonder about a dress representing Paris... A black lace cocktail dress: timelessly elegant like this city", he ends.

250

"I like wandering
and watching the Parisians
in their daily life."

Antoine Coysevox's **equestrian statue** represents "the fame of the king, riding the horse Pegasus". It's currently shield at the Louvre, whereas a copy is placed in place de la Concorde, nearby the Jardin des Tuileries entrance.

The **Four Seasons George V Hotel** *penthouse* suite is provided with a private terrace that has an enchanting view of Paris and its monuments, as the Eiffel Tower and the Cathedral Church of the Holy Trinity (American Cathedral in Paris).

Nymphs statues decorate **Bridge Alexander III** arcades.

# Author

**Alessandra Mattanza**, author, screenwriter and fine-art photographer, was born in Italy but has lived abroad for more than twenty years. She grew up in Australia and regularly goes back there for professional and personal reasons. She worked as an editor for the publisher Handelsblatt in Munich. She has lived in New York for several years and recently she has splitted herself between New York and Los Angeles. She loves wandering in Paris for work and pleasure. Her great passion for cinema has led her to specialize in interviews with actors and directors, as well as in traveling and fiction. She currently works as a foreign correspondent, contributor and editor for several publishers in Italy and Germany, including Rizzoli, Hearst, Mondadori, Sperling & Kupfer, Condé Nast, Cairo Editore, White Star/National Geographic/ De Agostini, and Giunti/Feltrinelli. Besides novels, she writes screenplays, tourist guides, coffee table and travel books, focusing her attention on the greatest cities in the world, cinema, music, animals and nature. In 2014 she won the "First Place for 2013" in "Personality Profile - International Journalism" at the 56th Annual Southern California Journalism Awards in Los Angeles. In 2015 she accomplished the screenplay based on her novel "Storie di New York" (Stories of New York, 2010) together with the American screenwriter Lucy Ridolphi. For Edizioni White Star Publishers she published "Australia. The New Frontier", "Wonders of New York", and "My New York: Celebrities Talk About the City".

The author wants to thank Bianca Guez for editing and the French translation,
as well as for her precious assistance in Paris; Julien Bardou and Caroline Ebke for their help during
the interview to Isabelle Huppert; Icelandic Air for the flight; reiki master Filippo Conte
for his fundamental support and Fabien Marcantetti for having welcomed her in Paris.

# Photographic Credits

All the texts and interviews have been approved
by the people Alessandra Mattanza interviewed.
To be as accurate as possible all the interviewees
have been asked to read and approve every text-interview
for publication. We apologize for any inaccurate
information and welcome corrections,
which will be made in future editions.

WHITE STAR PUBLISHERS

WS White Star Publishers® is a registered trademark
property of White Star s.r.l.

© 2016 White Star s.r.l.
Piazzale Luigi Cadorna, 6
20123 Milan, Italy
www.whitestar.it

Translation and Editing: TperTradurre s.r.l.

ISBN 978-88-544-1067-1
1 2 3 4 5 6   20 19 18 17 16

Printed in Croatia